Linguistics and Literature

To Norman Denison

Linguistics and Literature

An introduction to literary stylistics

Raymond Chapman

Senior Lecturer in English, London School of Economics and Political Science

Edward Arnold

© Raymond Chapman, 1973

First published 1973
by Edward Arnold (Publishers) Ltd.,
25 Hill Street, London W1X 8LL

Cloth edition ISBN: 0 7131 5685 6
Paper edition ISBN: 0 7131 5686 4

Printed in Great Britain by
T. & A. Constable Ltd., Edinburgh

Contents

Preface

This book is addressed to those who are interested, as students, teachers or general readers, in literature or linguistics. Its aim is to add them to the increasing number of people who are interested in both and have found that the two disciplines can illuminate one another in many ways. It is an introductory study, which does not pretend to give all the answers; indeed, stylistic criticism does not encourage anyone to claim to know all the answers. What is attempted here is a presentation of some possible methods of approach to the basic problems. Learning to ask the right sorts of question is perhaps the most important part of an academic training.

I am grateful to my colleagues Norman Denison, Jean Aitchison and David Durkin for advice on some points of linguistics. Elizabeth Johnson and Betty Smale have bravely tackled the vagaries of my handwriting and typing. The staff of the London Library are often thanked in prefaces for their helpfulness; I should like to add to the list.

Note on Reading

Although literary stylistics is still a comparatively new study, a great deal of work in this field has been published and any suggestions for further reading must necessarily be selective. Each chapter is followed by a list of books and essays which are particularly relevant to the topics which have just been discussed. Much important work is to be found in periodicals; but as many of these are specialist journals not likely to be accessible to all readers, reference has been made only to articles which have later been included in books.

The serious student will need to consult a full bibliography such as:

R. W. Bailey and D. M. Burton, *English Stylistics* (Cambridge, Mass., 1968, Massachusetts Institute of Technology Press).

L. T. Milic, *Style and Stylistics* (London, 1967, Collier-Macmillan).

The following books, which are frequently mentioned in the text and reading lists, are identified by one or two words in italics:

Chatman: Essays – S. Chatman and S. R. Levin, eds., *Essays on the Language of Literature* (Boston, 1967, Houghton Mifflin).

Chatman: Style – S. Chatman, ed., *Literary Style: a Symposium* (London, 1971, Oxford University Press).

Fowler – R. Fowler, ed., *Essays on Style and Language* (London, 1966, Routledge and Kegan Paul).

Leech – G. N. Leech, *A Linguistic Guide to English Poetry* (London, 1969, Longmans).

Minnis – N. Minnis, ed., *Linguistics at Large* (London, 1971, Gollancz).

Nowottny – W. Nowottny, *The Language Poets Use* (London, 1962, Athlone Press).

Allies or Opponents?

One of the problems raised by the linguistic theory of Noam Chomsky is the status of sentences like this:

> Colourless green ideas sleep furiously.

Here we have a sequence of words which must be accounted 'acceptable' English on grammatical criteria, since it responds to analysis by any reasonable method of classification, but which can hardly be seen as an 'acceptable' part of meaningful discourse in known varieties of English as a communicating language. It is difficult to find a context in which that particular utterance could be used.

Students of literature may respond differently to a sentence that deviates from the expectations of everyday usage. The sentence quoted above is not too remote from the type of language in which we learn to accept, and even to admire, indicative statements such as:

> Her fist of a face died clenched on a round pain
> (Dylan Thomas, 'In Memory of Ann Jones')

or:

> No, I'll not, carrion comfort, Despair, not feast on thee
> (Hopkins, 'Carrion Comfort')

in which the grammar follows a 'normal' pattern but in which scarcely any of the form-words are associated in familiar ways.

Again, Chomsky and his followers have been much concerned with the problem of ambiguity in linguistic statements. It is apparent that the earlier method of IC analysis (see p. 7) does not help to give an unequivocal meaning for the sentence:

> The police were ordered to stop drinking after midnight.

which has four possible interpretations that can be sorted out only by a deep analysis leading perhaps to rephrasing. In our everyday use of language we rightly regard such uncertainty of meaning as undesirable and do our best to avoid it. Yet critics continue to argue about the interpretation of the last lines of Keats's 'Ode on a Grecian Urn':

> When old age shall this generation waste,
> Thou shalt remain, in midst of other woe
> Than ours, a friend to man, to whom thou say'st,
> Beauty is truth, truth beauty,—that is all
> Ye know on earth, and all ye need to know.

What exactly is the Urn supposed to be 'saying'—the phrase 'Beauty is truth, truth beauty', followed by the poet's own comment, or the whole of the last two lines? In the absence of quotation marks from the original edition, we may be in doubt. The argument must certainly take into account the question whether Keats elsewhere uses 'ye' as a singular pronoun. The point is that the uncertainty is a source of stimulating discussion, adding to the interest of the whole poem rather than detracting from it.

There exists, then, a type of discourse in which we can apply evaluative words like 'clever', 'interesting', and even 'brilliant' to usage which might evoke very different adjectives if it occurred in a different situation. We may justify such discrimination by assigning Thomas, Hopkins and Keats to the realm of 'literature' when we are discussing certain written texts which they have left to posterity. The same tolerance might not extend to other aspects of their writing, such as their letters or their critical essays, and would certainly not be extended to an encounter with them in polite conversation if such were possible—though in practice we might carry over some of the respect attached to their literary reputation.

What is literature? The question may find an answer, or rather a number of answers, as we examine some specimens of language in the course of this book. At this stage it is easier to say what literature is not. First, it is not simply that which is written as opposed to that which is spoken. It is true that we speak loosely about the 'literature' which a manufacturer sends out to promote his product. Yet none of us would include such areas when considering the possible scope of a syllabus in English Literature. Nor would we include recipe books, telephone directories, Acts of Parliament or guidebooks to ancient buildings, though all of these are written and may be of interest for the study of language in general.

The distinction is not always quite so clear. If *Pilgrim's Progress* is counted as literature, what about Hobbes's *Leviathan*? Is Matthew Arnold's *Culture and Anarchy* literature as unquestionably as is his poetry? There is not likely to be a perfect test of admissibility to determine all cases; rather a spectrum of linguistic utterance, at one end of which are specimens of undisputed literature, at the other a much larger corpus that cannot be so labelled. There will always be an area of doubt and it need not greatly trouble us. Two features perhaps will be noticeable in those works which form a society's literature in the more specialized sense of the word. One is the interest attaching to the writer's choice of framework for the discourses which together make up his extant work. He will have used a method of organizing and connecting what he wants to say on a particular topic, generally in a unit which other writers have used and which critics have labelled as the species and sub-species known as *genres*. We approach a writer as a novelist or a dramatist or a poet, with narrower categories in mind—lyric, epic, elegy and so on. There are dangers that these labels will become artificial and restrictive, imposing a rigidity which is not inherent in the work itself; and of course many writers have practised different *genres*. Nevertheless, there is a special interest attaching to Bunyan's choice of prose allegory for *Pilgrim's Progress*, and Milton's choice of epic verse for *Paradise Lost*, which does not attach to the fact that textbooks are written in referential prose.

The other distinguishing feature of literature brings in a word which has been given many interpretations: 'imagination'. For the moment it is sufficient to say that the meaning is not confined to that of fantasy or even to the creation of characters and episodes which never had a 'real' existence. It means that the linguistic utterance which involves imagination has a quality beyond the use of words to convey referential meaning. A work of literature may indeed offer information; it may, and probably will, have a meaningful content which can be paraphrased in referential prose. But such a paraphrase will certainly seem 'less' than the original; it will have 'lost' something, it will be 'poorer'. The search for the positive quality implied by those negative words is an important part of literary criticism.

Literature, then, seems to offer language which is different from what may be loosely termed the 'normal' or 'everyday' usage of a speech-community, yet which is intelligible to the members of that community if they are willing to apply a special standard of acceptability. Literary language has been chosen and manipulated by its user with greater care and complexity than the average language-user either can or wishes to exercise. If this distinctive use is recognized, it may be possible to discuss intelligently a writer's individual 'style'.

These are questions to which we must return in more depth. Even in these general terms, they seem to limit the study of language to a particular area, and thus to deny the omnivorous appetite for data shown by modern linguistics. The question 'what is linguistics?' may be answered more precisely than the equivalent question about literature, but it cannot be fully answered in a few words. Readers of this book will probably have some basic knowledge of linguistics. For those who have not, the books listed at the end of this chapter will prove helpful. Briefly, the study of linguistics is concerned with language as an observable phenomenon of human activity, both in its general principles and in the particular realizations which we call 'languages'—English, French, Malay, Arabic and so on.

Clearly, literature is created from the basic material of linguistic study and is allied to it in a way that the other arts like music and painting are not. Yet it would be a sad error to regard linguistics as valuable only in connection with the study of literature. Linguists are interested in every form of language use, and also in the underlying 'rules' which govern potential as well as actual use. Literature occupies only a very small area of the total language map, and we have already found reason to suppose that it is a rather unusual area.

Should the linguist then eschew the literary creations of a language? This attitude tended to prevail during the founding period of modern linguistics. Ferdinand de Saussure, with his insistence on the primacy of everyday speech, was little interested in the written language and even less in the specifically literary: in his view, they were special uses which were comparatively unimportant in the study of language as a whole. His pupil Charles Bally, who began the systematic study of what we now call 'stylistics', again gave scant attention to literature.

Leonard Bloomfield, while paying a scholar's respects to the cultural value of literature, did not value it highly as a field of linguistic investigation; it deviated too much from the common denominator and was tainted with the association of classical philology which the new linguistics was trying to leave behind. Bloomfield's words are worth quoting since some linguists would still subscribe to them:

> The linguist . . . studies the language of all persons alike; the individual features in which the language of a great writer differs from the ordinary speech of his time and place interest the linguist no more than the individual features of any other person's speech, and much less than the features that are common to all speakers.
>
> (*Language*, pp. 21-2)

When those words were written, the study of linguistics was still fighting for its autonomy and needed to emphasize in what respects it differed from traditional language studies. Today most of the early anxieties have been outgrown and linguists are ready to re-open the frontiers that were closed in defence. The tools of linguistics can be used in related disciplines without reducing linguistics itself to a mere technology or service-station.

The literature of a language offers a corpus of material for linguistic study. It is, as we shall see, deviant in some respects from the more orthodox field of the linguist's concern. It is mostly written; it is mostly of the past; and it presents features peculiar to itself which are not found in other areas of expression. The more important consideration is that literature is the work of men who were specially sensitive to the language of their time and who used the skill of language to make permanent their vision of life. They manipulated language to make it contain a unique series of experiences and interpretations. That, surely, is enough reason for bringing every available scholarly skill to bear on its elucidation.

Co-operation without suspicion is needed from the literary scholar as well. Despite the outstanding critical work done in recent years by writers with both literary and linguistic training, there is still a general disapproval of linguistics when it impinges on literary subjects. It is regarded as 'too scientific'; its mathematical diagrams and terminology, its development of theory from empirical observation, its refusal to be prescriptive about 'good' or 'bad' usage, all serve to alienate the more traditional literary scholar. Yet some of these approaches are precisely what criticism needs for its continuing vitality.

This does not mean that all other critical approaches must be cast aside in the euphoria of what is new. The kind of study on which we are going to embark does not yield the whole truth about literature. Nevertheless, it is literary criticism and not some strange, improper use of literary material. It is a proper concern of literary study, but not the total concern. Frank Palmer has put the point in words which seem to me to admit no refutation:

> No linguist should ever hope to explain the aesthetic values of literature by linguistic investigation any more than the values of great music can be explained simply by a careful examination of the score. But literature no less than everyday speech is language and as such is a proper subject for linguistic investigation, even if there are some who would regard the linguistic analysis of a poem as a kind of blasphemy.
>
> (*Minnis*, p. 252)

We shall go on therefore in the belief that students of literature and of linguistics have each something to gain from that which was once considered to be the other's province. This book does not set out to be a survey of either linguistics or literary-critical methods, but rather to suggest the kind of investigation which may be helpful to both disciplines. It must be remembered that, although linguistics is now an autonomous discipline, it is not a homogeneous one. There are many schools, theories and methodologies; probably no linguist is fully acquainted with all of them and certainly no attempt can be made to represent each of them here. I shall work mainly on the assumptions which are common throughout the world of linguistic study, and if some ways of approach are particularly useful for literary texts they can be used without prejudice to their status in that world.

Samuel Johnson offered two reasons for not issuing a list of subscribers to his edition of Shakespeare: one was that he had lost all the names, the other that he had spent all the money. I can offer two different but equally cogent reasons for the fact that most of the examples used in this book are drawn from English literature. One is that they will be familiar, or at least comprehensible, to everyone who can read the book. The second is, very simply, that English is the only literature with which I can claim a more than superficial acquaintance. But I believe that the approaches will be valid, *mutatis mutandis*, for other literatures as well.

One more *caveat* before embarking on the real business. The end-product of literature, the text, is always capable of linguistic investigation. By definition, literature is the art that uses language. The starting-point, however, may be quite different. It may be a historical occasion, an emotional experience, a desire to rebuke and reform society. It may be a pattern of metre, or a sequence of sounds, or a collocation which cannot be regarded as an analysable linguistic utterance until it has been developed, or an image first presented to the visual sense. Ted Hughes has thus described a poem:

> An assembly of living parts moved by a single spirit. The living parts are the words, the images, the rhythms. The spirit is the life which inhabits them when they all work together. It is impossible to say which comes first, parts or spirit.[1]

Spirits cannot be confined: but they can be investigated.

FURTHER READING

Although this book is intended to give no difficulty to those who are not linguistic specialists, it makes no pretence to be a course in linguistics. Readers to whom the subject is completely new would do well to read David Crystal, *What is Linguistics?* (2nd edn., London, 1969, Edward Arnold) and to follow it with Crystal's longer book *Linguistics* (Harmondsworth, 1971, Penguin Books) or F. Palmer, *Grammar* (Harmondsworth, 1971, Penguin Books); both of the latter deal with IC (Immediate Constituent) Analysis which was referred to on p. 1.

Those who want to go beyond these introductory works will probably be taking a course of instruction and receiving advice on reading; for any who are relying on private study, the appropriate book is J. Aitchison, *Teach Yourself General Linguistics* (London, 1972, English Universities Press).

The outstanding figures in modern linguistics can be approached through their own work:

F. de Saussure, *Cours de Linguistique générale* (1916); English translation, *Course in General Linguistics* (London, 1960, Peter Owen).

E. Sapir, *Language* (New York, 1921, Harcourt Brace).

L. Bloomfield, *Language* (London, 1935 and 1950, Allen and Unwin).

---

[1] *Poetry in the Making* (London, 1967, Faber and Faber), p. 17.

N. Chomsky, *Syntactic Structures* (The Hague, 1957, Mouton) and *Aspects of the Theory of Syntax* (Cambridge, Mass., 1965, Massachusetts Institute of Technology Press); Chomsky's books, especially the second, are not easy and should not be attempted before reading one or more of the introductory works mentioned above. A good simplified explanation of his theories is J. Lyons, *Chomsky* (London, 1970, Collins).

The issues raised in this chapter are discussed by G. Steiner, 'Linguistics and Literature' (*Minnis*, pp. 113-36); M. A. K. Halliday, 'The Linguistic Study of Literary Texts' (*Chatman: Essays*, pp, 217-23); R. Jakobson, 'Linguistics and Poetics' (*Chatman: Essays*, pp. 296-322); R. Fowler, 'Linguistic Theory and the Study of Literature' (*Fowler*, pp. 1-29).

Readers with special interest in English studies who want a linguistic approach without going too deeply into general linguistics should read R. Quirk, *The Use of English* (London, 1962, Longman), followed by H. A. Gleason, *Linguistics and English Grammar* (New York, 1965, Holt, Rinehart and Winston).

2

Literature and Stylistics

The word 'language' is not easily defined without reference to the context in which it is used. Consider these four sentences, each of which could be constructed and understood without difficulty by a native speaker of English:

> All human beings possess the power of language.
> Latin is a synthetic language.
> We were delighted by the old man's homely language.
> Contracts should be drawn up in proper legal language.

It is clear that in each of these sentences 'language' is made to cover a different area of reference. This kind of indeterminacy causes little trouble in everyday conversation but is unacceptable in serious linguistic study where a more precise division of the area is necessary.

Linguists have generally adopted the terminology of de Saussure, who used *langage* to describe the faculty of human speech in general, *langue* for the totality of a particular language-system and *parole* for an act of speech by an individual user of that system. We need not consider all the axioms and definitions on which he based his theory. There is no problem in accepting *langue* as the total resources available to anyone who is a member of a speech-community and shares with others a system which can be given a name such as English, or French, or Korean, or Tagalog. Information about *langue* is collected in dictionaries, grammar-books and studies of pronunciation. That which is observed for the compilation of these books is *parole*—or rather, enough examples of *parole* to allow the formation of general rules. A similar distinction is that made by Chomsky between 'competence' and 'performance', and the need for these distinctions becomes apparent as soon as we think seriously about the subject.

Saussure's descriptions could be respectively substituted for the

B

word 'language' in each of the first three sentences above. The fourth sentence uses 'language' with reference not to any specific utterance but to an abstraction within the wider system. The notion of 'legal language', 'medical language', 'religious language' is familiar enough, but what exactly does it mean? The abstraction is composed from a large number of *paroles* in which certain linguistic features recur with high enough frequency to be significant. Each of these 'languages' is unquestionably part of a certain *langue*, showing enough common features to be intelligible in general pattern, if not in every detail, to most users of that *langue*.

No special linguistic skill is required to pick out some of these recurrent features. In English legal documents, for instance, we may be struck by the high incidence of conjunctional phrases—'without let or hindrance', 'the messuage or dwelling-house', 'the last will and testament'; and a little work with the dictionary will show that these often contain a word of Old English origin linked with one of Romance origin. When we speak of 'religious language' we are probably thinking of the Book of Common Prayer and the Authorized Version of the Bible. Here we find similar linked phrases—'when we assemble and meet together', 'sore let and hindered', 'confirm and strengthen'. In the grammar of this 'language' we find the second person singular pronoun 'thou', with its oblique forms and the associated verbal inflection *-est* which is obsolete in most types of present-day English.

Similar observations can be made about more widespread communications. The average academic lecture will contain few or no direct imperatives, but a higher proportion of complex sentences than we should expect to hear in a conversation on the bus. News commentators on the broadcasting media have adopted the use of the simple present for a proximate future—'at the end of this bulletin we talk to a correspondent', 'we hear the views of people in the streets'.

The basis of such observations is the choice of certain linguistic features in place of others. From recognizing a greater frequency of these features than is found in other types of utterance, we can go on and analyse enough specimens to allow the formulation of a description. That which is described will be something that the non-linguist recognizes without analysis; something that can be parodied and imitated. The set of features which is accepted as fully appropriate in one situation may seem comic or distasteful if it occurs in another.

Instead of talking about 'legal language' and so on it is better to call these distinctive usages *styles*. The notion of 'legal style' or 'religious style' is, like all other attempts to categorize language, made possible by the performance of users. When a user directs his performance towards a particular style, he is adopting a *register*. The adoption of register may be deliberate and with awareness of a recognized style, as when a barrister speaks in court. When the same barrister speaks to his small children at home he will use a different register, one which is less formalized and more instinctive. (Most parents use a special register for children, despite frequent protestations to the contrary.)

Almost every individual has command of a number of registers which he uses in different situations of his life—at work, at home, with friends of his own age and sex, speaking at a public meeting and so on. Choice of register is constrained by the circumstances of communication rather than by the content. Many native users of English would give the same message in different forms according to their relationship with the recipient, for example:

> We hope to arrive at approximately four o'clock.
> We'll be there about four.
> We'll turn up fourish.

The common adoption of a register by a number of people in a certain recurring situation creates a style. An established style may make the use of appropriate register obligatory. It should be made clear that this use of the word 'register' is quite different from its use in music and phonetics to denote the scale of pitch covered by an instrument or voice.

The linguistic study of different styles is called *stylistics*. The foregoing description has shown that styles are the product of social situation: of a common relationship between language-users. Stylistics is thus a part of *sociolinguistics*—language studied in relation to society. Sociolinguists are interested in the effect upon language of speakers' groups according to ethnic, social, class or other divisions. Stylistic features may derive from more temporary associations as well, those which concern a speaker's working or leisure time only. But every style is used for communication within a group, large or small, close-knit or scattered, with features which are accepted as communicative by members of the group.

Now this is clearly something different from the use of 'style' in more traditional approaches to language. Literary critics and commentators on the quality of written language have made us so familiar with a certain conception of 'style' that it may be necessary to make a deliberate change in our thinking. 'Good style', or sometimes simply 'style', has been used as a description of writing that was in some way praiseworthy, skilful or elegant. Quiller-Couch remarked, 'Style in writing is much the same as good manners in other human intercourse.'[1]

This kind of evaluation need not be dismissed as unintelligent, but it is not the concern of linguistics to make these judgements. Its use to the student of literature is to provide techniques on which evaluative judgement can be based. In linguistic analysis, however, 'style' is not an ornament or a virtue; it is not something to be characterized as 'good' or 'bad' in any absolute sense. Nor is it confined to written language, or to literature, or to any single aspect of language. There is no use of language that is not open to stylistic investigation. Some areas, however, are richer in material for such investigation because they show a high incidence of special features.

Instead of a dogmatic evaluation of any linguistic specimen as 'good' or 'bad', it is more reasonable to consider to what style it belongs and then to ask whether its features are appropriate to that style as commonly observed. We return to the point that the same referential content may be expressed in different ways. If someone says, 'The sun is rising', we accept his statement as one appropriate to most conversational situations. We accept the message and are unlikely to give conscious attention to the mode of communication. Yet there are other ways of expressing the same point which will make us more aware of manner as well as matter.

> The diffused daylight which precedes the passage of the sun above the horizon is due to refraction, reflection, and scattering of the light of the sun by the atmosphere.

> But look, the morn, in russet mantle clad,
> Walks o'er the dew of yon high eastern hill.

In meeting either of these statements, we recognize the presence of something more than the 'common core' of the language. Either of

[1] A. T. Quiller-Couch, *The Art of Writing* (Cambridge, 1916, Cambridge University Press).

them would probably cause mirth or embarrassment if it came out in colloquial conversation. The first, however, would be acceptable in a style generally described as 'scientific'; the second is recognized, with detached tolerance or deep involvement according to personal predispositions, as 'literary'. Recognition of style is primary; other questions may follow.

Stylistics, then, is not confined to literature, although its application to literature is the concern of this book. In some respects, literature is the most difficult type of language to approach stylistically, because of the diversity and complexity which will appear in the course of investigation. The difficulty is more than compensated by the special value of the material being investigated. At this stage we may indeed admit a concept of quality and excellence, which can be scrutinized by the more objective criteria of linguistics.

Yet can we really think of literature as a style? Is there a discernible literary style, as there is a legal or liturgical style? Obviously literature is not confined to any aspect of human experience, nor does it exclude any. Within a given *langue*, any *parole* could be incorporated into the literature using that *langue*. Literary style is not something to be described by a few salient characteristics; but careful study of literary texts will show that literary stylistics is a viable study. Like all meaningful use of *langue*, literature contains a great deal of 'common core' which would cause no surprise in any situation. It also contains a higher incidence of special or deviant features than non-literary styles. Between these extremes, it is possible to observe that literary style shows more careful and consistent use of the regular patterns of the language: the 'rules' of traditional grammar, which drew examples from literature because of its regularity as much as its prestige. As we shall see, much of the most striking literary language appears deviant when it is really using, with singular economy and compression, the resources available to all native speakers.

To say that literary language is more careful is another way of saying that it is more conscious in formation. Literature uses language as an artistic medium, not simply for communication or even expression. It is not spontaneous, whatever theories of spontaneous inspiration may sometimes have been canvassed. It is considered and developed in a way that is impossible for everyday conversation, or even for the more deliberate registers adopted for certain styles.

While other styles show recurrent features, literature is distinguished by what can be described overall as *pattern*. The text will show selection and arrangement of items that contribute to the total effect; elements that would be absent or incidental in other styles are important for the fulfilment of purpose. Poetry shows such patterning devices as metre, rhyme, assonance, alliteration; prose may contain similar devices, less regularly arranged. Both types of literary discourse will have careful and often unexpected selection of words and syntactic constructions. Figures of rhetoric will give unusual prominence to certain items. We may therefore add a third to the two distinguishing marks of literature suggested in the previous chapter: the use of special devices which heighten the effect of linguistic acts through patterning.

Literature may be much more than would normally be understood as a 'style', but there is value in attempting to treat it as one. Any profitable approach through linguistics must deal with literature as an examinable part of the available realization of *langue*. Special, heightened and prestigious as it may be, it cannot deviate too far from the expectations of the speech-community if it is to find any readers at all. Such deviations as occur can be discerned and described by methods applicable to more familiar and humbler *paroles*. Like other styles, it has features not shared by all users at all levels; but, as in all styles, these features can be utilized only in association with 'common core' features.

Extremes are generally dangerous and distorting. In some periods and cultures literary language has gained such prestige that other styles have been judged good or bad according to their resemblance to it. Non-literary users have tried to incorporate literary features into personal communication. The development of national languages has been affected by the prestige of a dialect used for literature; individual writers have left their mark on common speech. This kind of influence, by no means undesirable in itself, has had the unfortunate effect of isolating literature from regular methods of investigation. The other extreme, which has already been mentioned, was the dismissal of literature by some modern linguists as too deviant for their attention.

It is now generally accepted that any description of a *langue* must take account of all its different realizations. The present investigation sees literary style as deriving its strength from the 'common core', even in respect of features which are usually thought to be distinctively 'literary'. Its deviations do not break down communication with 'common core' users. Certainly it is sometimes necessary to make the kind of adjustment or allowance which in the past was vaguely named 'poetic licence'. At the same time, the very extension of literature into all aspects of human experience means that its style is less exclusive than some others which are the preserves of smaller groups.

The literary writers have themselves been divided about the particularity of their style. The course of English poetry, for instance, shows a succession of swings between belief in the special nature of poetic diction and insistence that the criterion of poetic greatness was its closeness to everyday speech. At the end of the sixteenth century, Spenser tended to the first view and Donne to the second. Restoration poets in turn reacted against the school of Donne, which seemed to have become artificial and remote from real life. Most eighteenth-century poets shared the opinion of Gray that 'the language of the age is never the language of poetry', until Wordsworth came with his standard of poetry written from 'a selection of language really used by men'.

One task of literary stylistics is, without taking sides in this dispute, to determine how far and in what respects a poet's language in fact shows deviant features. Another is to note how a writer uses generally accepted features to special effect. It is necessary to pay close attention to particular writers, since literature shows far more diversity of individual usage than do other styles. This fact creates a link between modern stylistics and the more traditional way of discussing a writer's style in the sense of the too-often quoted dictum of Buffon—'Le style est l'homme même'.

Although we have tried to postulate a literary style, as parallel to a legal, medical or religious style, it is apparent that we are led to someting that is far from being homogeneous. In practice, the examination of a single writer, or of the common features of a school or literary period showing common aims and influences, will yield the most satisfactory results. Whatever can realistically be said about literary style as a whole is worth saying as a contribution to critical theory and to understanding of how language works. In the present study, examples from particular writers will be used as evidence for general principles, but the aim of the whole is to prepare readers for close stylistic study of more limited areas.

Unlike other styles, literature does not and cannot exclude any aspects of *langue*. Here the notion of register is important to stylistics, as we approach the writer as an individual user of resources potentially available to other members of the speech-community. Like other users, he is in a relationship of communication, though one of monologue rather than dialogue. The reciprocal attitudes of writers and readers towards one another is an important part of the sociology of literature and naturally enters into stylistics. Each writer will in fact choose registers according to varying factors in the situation.

The limiting factors may be mentioned first, although they generally produce less interesting results. Like other styles, literature may constrain an individual to adopt a particular register. Prescriptive forces tend to operate in literary culture, not always of the same kind or of the same intensity. Even periods of revolt, like the Romantic movement, bring their own inhibitions and pressures to replace the old. The totally permissive society is no more a reality in literature than in human organization as a whole. Sometimes the pressures are more overt and more clearly codified, as in the negative attitude to poetic diction in the eighteenth century, which objected to certain words and phrases as foreign, technical, or too common-place in their associations. There was a positive pressure as well, in the attempt to prescribe words specially or solely suitable for poetic expression. Johnson tended towards the first attitude and Addison towards the second, while Pope fought in both camps.

To some extent, then, the critics and writers of literature may create a style which demands that a certain register be adopted, others avoided, by those who seek acceptability within the group of style-conformists. The rules seldom endure for a long period of time, since those who break them can equally claim to have incorporated their register into a new literary style. Whether his attitude to prevailing fashion be one of acquiescence or of rebellion, however, a writer is unlikely to stick to any single register for the whole of his literary output. It is the business of literary stylistics to recognize and examine the different registers encountered.

A writer will perhaps change in this as he changes his attitude to the currently prestigious literary style. There will be other reasons too for the adoption of different registers. He may be aware of addressing different groups of readers, as a speaker changes register in moving from one set of acquaintances to another. Examples can be seen in books written specifically for children by authors who have generally worked at the adult level. Compare the narrative of Kingsley's *The Heroes* or of Dickens's *Child's History of England* with that of their novels, and note such features as more direct second-person address, shorter sentences, a smaller range of lexical items. Sometimes the difference of register will be linked with difference of *genre* or literary kind, as when Donne's sermons are compared with his poetry. The sermon, although 'literary' in some features, will draw from the religious style and from the oratorical. Its direct address is different from the assumption of an interlocutory *persona* in the lyric.

Yet this latter assumption, widely adopted by poets, brings register-change. The imaginary critic or questioner may be made to speak in a way that heightens by contrast the poet's own address to the reader. Such are the interpolations of 'Arbuthnot' in Pope's *Prologue to the Satires* and the hearty indictment that begins Housman's apologia in no. LXII of *A Shropshire Lad*:

> 'Terence, this is stupid stuff:
> You eat your victuals fast enough;
> There can't be much amiss, 'tis clear,
> To see the rate you drink your beer.
> But oh, good Lord, the verse you make,
> It gives a chap the belly-ache . . .'

and so on, with colloquial contractions of auxiliaries, near-clichés such as 'fast enough', lexical items like 'belly-ache' seldom found in the literary style, and reference to physical activity. At last the poet starts to reply in the same register and then turns to a more formal narrative conclusion without second-person reference which lifts his poetry as a whole into a different world from the common-sense standard of 'victuals' and 'beer':

> There was a king reigned in the East:
> There, when kings will sit to feast,
> They get their fill before they think
> With poisoned meat and poisoned drink.
> He gathered all that springs to birth
> From the many-venomed earth . . .
> I tell the tale that I heard told.
> Mithridates, he died old.

A similar register-change may be observed in the novel written in the first person. Consider the 'adult', sophisticated and ironical register of the narrator in *David Copperfield*, contrasted with the child's speech of the remembered boy-David; or the mature Butler's *persona* Overton reporting the conversation of Ernest Pontifex as child and undergraduate.

The novel and the drama must use a number of registers since they still 'contain' characters conceived as beings of separate existence communicating in an imaginary but recognizable society. It is no novelty in literary criticism to study how the most skilful writers clearly differentiate the speech of their characters, while the incompetent or unpractised make no significant variation; stylistic study considers how these effects are made. The question of written dialogue introduces the idea of *dialect*—the distinctive system of a group of users of a *langue*, with common regional or class identity. Here, writing so clearly interprets speech that more consideration must be given to it in a later chapter. Finally, the speeches attributed to a character in literature will yield samples of an imaginary *idiolect*—the choice from *langue* made by an individual at a given stage in his life. The stylistic investigator may compare a fictional or dramatic idiolect with examples drawn from real speakers of similar age, class, education or region, and may thus offer some serious evidence for the frequent discussion of whether a character is or is not 'true to life'.

A fruitful subject for stylistic study is the deliberate mixing of registers without clear identification of speakers; the shift of utterance is marked by shift of register and not by any extraneous pointers. Such mixing, generally frowned upon in the past as an offence against *decorum*, is widely used in recent and current literature. If we met the 'scientific' description of dawn, previously quoted, in a work which we had accepted as 'literary', we might suppose a deliberate contrast for ironic or other effect. For the modern reader is habituated to the raiding of other registers, which Joyce carried out in *Ulysses* and Eliot in *The Waste Land*. The complexity of society, the uncertainty of personal identity, the realization of coinherence in a common human predicament—all this can be suggested through the changing viewpoints shown by selection of different register-features.

An example of mixed registers, which has been noticed by other critics but is too good not to use, is Henry Reed's poem, 'Naming of Parts'. Here no typographical devices show the transition to and fro between the words of the army instructor and the thought-observations of the poet-recruit. All is done by linguistic placing and selection, with use of the clichés from the teaching manual familiar to thousands of soldiers, switching to the kind of language expected from a literate and imaginative user. The sexual imagery drawn from the ambivalence in some of the instructional items points a contrast between the sterile destructiveness of war and the natural life-force. The first and the last two stanzas must serve to illustrate:

Today we have naming of parts. Yesterday,
We had daily cleaning. And tomorrow morning
We shall have what to do after firing. But today,
Today we have naming of parts. Japonica
Glistens like coral in all of the neighbouring gardens,
    And today we have naming of parts. . . .

And this you can see is the bolt. The purpose of this
Is to open the breech, as you see. We can slide it
Rapidly backwards and forwards: we call this
Easing the spring. And rapidly backwards and forwards
The early bees are assaulting and fumbling the flowers:
    They call it easing the Spring.

They call it easing the Spring: it is perfectly easy
If you have any strength in your thumb: like the bolt,
And the breech, and the cocking-piece, and the point of
                    balance,
Which in our case we have not got; and the almond-blossom
Silent in all the gardens and the bees going backwards and
                    forwards,
For today we have naming of parts.

The full potential of the *langue* can be indicated in a short extra-polation from different registers. The critic who uses stylistic method needs to be aware of the potentiality and to be able to recognize the styles and registers available to the literary writer. Apart from the kind of proscription imposed by convention, the writer is free to select from *langue* where he will, aided by his peculiar sensitivity to the use of language. The critic should try to respond with equal freedom, with as much sensitivity as he can claim, and with knowledge of the basic material from which literature is made.

FURTHER READING

An examination of what is meant by 'style' in modern linguistics could well begin with N. E. Envist, J. Spencer and M. J. Gregory, *Linguistics and Style* (London, 1964, Oxford University Press). The principal styles of present-day English are surveyed in D. Davy and D. Crystal, *Investigating English Style* (London, 1969, Longman).

On register, dialect and idiolect see also C. Barber, *Linguistic Change in Present-day English* (Edinburgh, 1964, Oliver and Boyd), pp. 16-33; A. E. Darbyshire, *A Description of English* (London, 1967, Edward Arnold), pp. 1-29 and 159-77; R. Quirk, 'Linguistic, Usage and the User' (*Minnis*, pp. 297-313).

P. Guiraud, *La Stylistique* (5th edn., Paris, 1967, Presses Universitaires de France) is an interesting introduction by a French linguist.

Readers who want to go more deeply into sociolinguistics should start with P. P. Giglioli, ed., *Language and Social Context* (Harmondsworth, 1972, Penguin Books).

Discussions of the specific nature of literary language are many; the present-day debate owes much to I. A. Richards, *Principles of Literary Criticism* (London, 1924, Routledge and Kegan Paul). An important though less easily accessible book is I. Hungerland, *Poetic Discourse* (Berkeley and Los Angeles, 1958, California University Press). Valuable shorter discussions are *Nowottny*, pp. 1-25; *Leech*, pp. 1-19; B. Lee, 'The New Criticism and the Language of Poetry' (*Fowler*, pp. 29-52); A. L. Binns, 'Linguistic Reading: two suggestions of the quality of literature' (*Fowler*, pp. 118-34); J. C. Ransom, 'Wanted: an Ontological Critic' (*Chatman: Essays*, pp. 269-82).

Traditional views of poetic diction are surveyed by F. W. Bateson, *English Poetry and the English Language* (Oxford, 1934, Oxford University Press) and S. A. Leonard, *The Doctrine of Correctness in English Usage* (Madison, 1929, Wisconsin University Press).

Once the new understanding of 'style' has been reached readers will lose nothing and may well profit from reading some of the older, more prescriptive works such as H. W. and F. G. Fowler, *The King's English* (Oxford, 1906, Oxford University Press) and A. T. Quiller-Couch, *The Art of Writing* (Cambridge, 1916, Cambridge University Press).

A modern linguistic approach to correct usage is J. Warburg, *Verbal Values* (London, 1966, Edward Arnold).

3

Language, Literature and History

When applicants for a university course in linguistics are asked about their motives they very often say that they are interested in the development of language. They want to learn more about 'how words change their meanings', 'the history of English grammar', or 'the influence of Anglo-Saxon'. They have to be gently told that these matters are not among the primary concerns of modern linguistics. In nineteenth-century philology, historical study played a large part; the reaction against it was vigorous and perhaps more sweeping than we should wish to perpetuate.

Once again we can turn to Saussure for a fundamental explanation. He separated the *diachronic* study of language, which traces development through the past, from the *synchronic* view of the total state of a *langue* at a given point of time. The chosen point is usually that of present-day observation, and some linguists claim to have practically no concern with what happened in the past. Although historical linguistics is a respectable branch of the subject, it is a comparatively minor one.

Yet literature comes to us mainly from the past. There are good academic grounds for not attempting to study the literature of our own time without some knowledge of that which has gone before. An examination of literary style as it appears at the present day would certainly be both interesting and revealing, but if literary stylistics is to be of deeper value educationally or in personal appreciation, it must be effective for the literature of all periods. The stylistic study of a writer or school will be synchronic in its concern for total performance using the linguistic code available at the time. Diachronic considerations must enter as we look back from our present position: the code by which we formulate our reactions to literature and verbalize our judgements is not identical with the code understood by Chaucer, Shakespeare or Dryden, or even Browning.

The apparent conflict is not irreconcilable. Even Saussure recognized the intersection of synchronic and diachronic in every linguistic act. His concern was not to abolish diachronic study, but to avoid confusion of the two approaches. When we examine a literary text we are making a double extrapolation—from the time-axis of historical development and from the performance-axis of all accessible linguistic acts made at that point of time. Questions based on our knowledge of both axes must be asked; description of performance requires knowledge of code.

The critic needs to think clearly about this intersection. He will use the tools of modern linguistic scholarship without supposing that they were somehow present in the mind of a past writer—a supposition which is clearly absurd as soon as it is formulated but which has a way of being insidiously troublesome beneath the surface.

There is a possible analogy in the history of prices and wages, related to currency changes. Old records of payment can be converted to modern decimal currency which will give the student an idea of what things used to cost. Effective conversion needs two quite different skills. First, there is the ability to work in the old currency and see whether the accounts are accurate in their own terms—to discover whether the man who left the record had got his sums right. Secondly, the methods of economic history can help to relate former prices and wages in real terms and to show their significance for the wider considerations of society at that time in the past.

Working with the old currency is like using diachronic knowledge. Although linguistic performance does not yield to notions of right and wrong like a set of accounts, the accepted usage of society in any period produces its own rules. We need to know, as it were, the 'value' of words at a given time; the semantic equivalent in present-day speech may be discovered, as groats and shillings can be converted into decimal currency. The popular interest in 'how words change their meaning' in fact represents a real concern of stylistics. Semantic change can cause serious misunderstanding of what a writer was in fact trying to say. Evaluation of performance will not be helpful if it proceeds from the wrong starting-place.

Words in isolation are dangerous traps for aspiring linguists. Semantics is a difficult and still experimental branch of study, which finds little profit in single lexical items. Yet there are certain conversions that have to be made before closer analysis can begin.

When Johnson wrote of *Lycidas* that it was in 'the form of a pastoral: easy, vulgar and therefore disgusting', his opinion was literary and not moralistic. 'Easy' must be converted to 'over-simple', 'vulgar' to 'commonplace' and 'disgusting' to 'distasteful to refined literary sensibility', before any further comment can be attempted. Or when Sam Weller enquires about his 'mother-in-law' we may waste time looking for evidence that he was married unless we can make the immediate conversion to 'stepmother' and thus identify the character to whom he is referring.

Diachronic information is not confined to a glossary of changes in meaning. A glossary will be primarily concerned with the *denotations* of words. Full comprehension, in all styles and especially in litera-ture, depends on grasping the *connotations*—the emotive ambience of words, their associations and the emotions which they may arouse. It is simple enough to explain *thou* as the second person singular pronoun, subjective case, and to add that it is now archaic except in a few special registers. But this does not take us very far in a study of *Twelfth Night* when the text gives the advice of Sir Toby to Sir Andrew about how to convey a challenge to Viola, disguised as the young man Cesario:

> Taunt him with the licence of ink: if thou thou'st him some thrice, it shall not be amiss.

> (III. ii)

This seems very curious, so long as it is read only at the level of traditional grammar. Its effect depends on the social connotation of *thou* in that period. Sir Toby rightly uses it in speaking to his friend and equal Sir Andrew, but it would be a sharp insult for the latter to use it in writing to a mere acquaintance who seemed to be moving on the same social level. But the second *thou* is placed and inflected as a verb: is this some bold and unique device of Shakespeare's, which might seem too imaginative for the character of Sir Toby? Recourse to other contemporary evidence reveals both connotation and usage. When Edward Coke was conducting the prosecution of Ralegh for treason, he made the same insult in the same way:

> All that he did was at thy instigation, for I thou thee, thou traitor.

And Stubbes related of his wife that:

She was never heard to give the lie nor so much as to thou any in anger.

In this instance we have looked along the horizontal axis of Elizabethan and Jacobean English to establish a basis for criticism of a specific text. It is possible also to trace a particular item along the vertical axis of historical development. For instance, the form of the negative imperative normally used at the end of the sixteenth century is frequently exemplified in Shakespeare, as:

> No, faith, my coz, wish not a man from England
> > *(Henry V*, IV. iii)

> I love thee not, therefore pursue me not
> > *(A Midsummer Night's Dream*, II. ii)

By 1700 the auxiliary *do* was in general use for this construction, having grown from rarity (it appears a few lines after the first of the above quotations) to dominance. This change gives a standpoint for the criticism of Keats's *Ode to Melancholy*:

> No, no, go not to Lethe

and of Housman:

> Tell me not here, it needs not saying.

As time passes, the older construction becomes more remote so that its use in poetry is a conscious choice by the poet which stands apart from everyday discourse. Its function is no longer straightforward but suggests literary artifice by the exploitation of archaic usage with its traditional associations.

Examples from one more field of linguistics may serve to establish the need for a historical approach. Knowledge of phonology as a diachronic study will often correct false conclusions about rhymes which are no longer 'good' rhymes according to present-day Received Pronunciation:

> I'll tune thy elegies to trumpet-sounds
> And write thy epitaph in blood and wounds.
> > (Montrose)

> Here thou, great Anna! whom three realms obey,
> Dost sometimes counsel take—and sometimes tea.
> > (Pope)

In these and a great many other instances the poet produced a perfect rhyme. Change in the pronunciation of one of the rhyming words makes it appear to the modern reader as if there had been an incompetent or deliberate lapse from the pattern of the poem.

Although they are of little importance in the mainstream of present-day linguistics, these considerations are of the first import-ance to the student of literary stylistics. The existence of new and exciting developments in the subject as a whole may endanger the status of slightly less up-to-date approaches. Diachronic study does not divert research into unprofitable channels provided its limits are defined and observed. In literary stylistics, the linguist calls on the aid of historical research, just as in other branches of linguistics he calls on sociology or psychology or anthropology.

Using the resources of history in stylistic criticism confronts us with another and more closely linguistic question. What status do we afford to literary texts in relation to the language as a whole? Concentration on one style has the danger that it will come to be seen as the style with particular prestige by which others are to be judged. Until recently the literature of a culture was seen as the highest linguistic usage, as the level to which all utterances should aspire and by which they could be somehow graded. Appeal to the 'best authors' was the justification of lexicographers, grammarians and those who sought to teach 'style' in the old sense. The appeal was especially strong in Britain, where the absence of any kind of Academy meant that a weight of literary usage could be taken to justify a prescriptive rule. Great writers were, among their other excellences, models for imitation.

The notion of a model in this sense—as one might speak of a 'model answer' to an examination question—is not congenial to the spirit of modern linguistics. A more useful approach is the attempt to create a model in the more philosophical sense of a construct which adequately represents reality and serves for the explanation and evaluation of specific instances. It is possible to describe a model of language in this way, as the norm of usage acceptable to the native speakers in a given community at a given time. Due allowance is then made for the distinctive usages of different styles which depart to a greater or lesser extent from the common stock. In this perspective, the language of literature is often notably deviant.

The concept of deviation is an important one in stylistics and we shall return to it. It arises as soon as we set particular linguistic acts against the apparent norm and it appears in two ways. First, there

C

is the statistical deviation which would make Housman's 'Tell me not here' a minority usage in the corpus of late nineteenth-century standard English. A deviant feature, lexical, syntactic or phonological, can simply be noted as an infrequent item in the total. Stylistic study will seek to account for it and to judge its effect within the whole text. The significance of deviation may depend on the precision or delicacy with which the parameters are drawn. The same archaic form of the negative imperative would not be deviant in liturgical usage which perpetuates sixteenth-century English and yields such examples as 'lead us not into temptation', 'enter not into judgement', 'or else come not to that Holy Table'.

It is possible to recognize a second and more interesting kind of deviance in what appears to be the novel and distinctive usage of a particular writer. Shakespeare's use of the verb 'spanieled' could be statistically recorded as a single example not found elsewhere in the surviving evidence of Elizabethan English. What is more interesting is to regard it as an item devised for a particular context, using lexical, morphological and syntactic methods permitted by the norm but never before combined in that way: the substantive *spaniel*, the past tense verbal inflection *-ed* and the relative sentence-position generally given to a transitive verb, producing

> The hearts
> That spanieled me at heels, to whom I gave
> Their wishes.
>
> (*Antony and Cleopatra*, IV.xii)

There is no great difficulty here, nor in many other examples of deviation such as:

> The achieve of, the mastery of the thing
>
> (Hopkins)
>
> Once below a time I lordly had the trees and leaves
>
> (Thomas)

Yet as we go farther back in time, there is less and less evidence on which to base the judgement of norm and deviation. The concept is less useful for older than for more recent literature because it becomes more difficult to construct a model. So much of what has been preserved from earlier states of the language is literary that we cannot cast a survey wide enough to say what was normative.

There is also a danger that the attitude to literary language which sees it as mainly deviant can harden into a new kind of prescriptivism, with literature as a pathological condition of the language and common speech as the healthy norm. At one time it was possible to set examination questions asking for comments on such 'errors of grammar' by the masters as Shakespeare's 'Young Ferdinand, whom they suppose is drowned', or Byron's 'There let him lay'. Nowadays the crime is more likely to be that of deviation from the lowest common denominator.

With these caveats in mind, the idea of deviation can be an extremely useful approach to at least some kinds of literary language. Deviation is not a pejorative term if we maintain an objective view of the many possible styles. After due observation it is indeed valid to adjudge the deviation of the feeble-minded or the aphasic to be undesirable because it hinders communication, and the deviation of the poet commendable because it heightens awareness and understanding. Any such judgements must depend on a synchronic picture of language gained from adequate sampling of a given period.

Therefore the student of literary stylistics needs to go beyond the limits of 'literature' and 'non-literature', which we have already seen to be scarcely meaningful. The evidence already quoted for the connotation of Elizabethan *thou* is an example. Similarly, features of language which may appear to be specifically and solely literary may in fact be shared with other registers: sharing of features is not to be confused with the kind of deliberate borrowing from other registers which has been noticed. It is no doubt easy to find something stilted and artificial in Byron's:

> The angel of death spread his wings on the blast
> And breathed in the face of the foe as he passed . . .
> ('The Destruction of Sennacherib')

or in Evelyn Green's:

The angel of death had not come alone—there was Another with him.
(*Only a Child*)

Surely this is remote from any other use of language in the nineteenth century—totally deviant from what anyone could ever have spoken.

Yet here is John Bright, speaking in the House of Commons in 1855:

> The angel of death has been abroad through the land; you may almost hear the beating of his wings.

The interchange between literary and non-literary language is not confined to discrete features. We are accustomed, certainly in European cultures, to think of a 'standard' form of a national language, local or class variants on it being regarded as dialects. In many instances, however, the standard form is traceable back to a dialect which gained prestige through being the medium of literature. A period of great literary production, with associated confidence in execution, can elevate a dialect to superior status and cause it to be adopted by educated members of the community for written and—usually later—for spoken communication, without area restriction. This status was gained by West Saxon in pre-Conquest England and by East Midland at the beginning of the fifteenth century. The same kind of thing happened to Francien in France, Castilian in Spain and Tuscan in Italy. In all these instances, economic and social factors also played their part; it can be argued that the literature of these dialects owed its strength to favourable external conditions. Luther's choice of Saxon can certainly be seen to have a direct influence on the development of German, partly through the deliberate aid of later writers and grammarians. Without over-simplifying a complex question, it is important to realize that literature helps to affect the diachronic development of the *langue* which is its medium. Ernst Cassirer's words are worth remembering:

> No poet can create an entirely new language. He has to adopt the words and he has to respect the fundamental rules of his language. To all this, however, the poet gives not only a new turn but also a new life ... The Italian language, the English language, the German language, were not the same at the death of Dante, of Shakespeare, of Goethe, as they had been at the day of their birth.[1]

Prestige, status and high quality are notions which are scarcely congenial to the more descriptive and analytical approach of modern linguistics, but which cannot be altogether excluded from

[1] *An Essay on Man* (New Haven, 1944, Yale University Press).

literary stylistics. Probably no one can make a useful study of literature without some sense of its excellence as a product of the human mind. The value of new methods depends on starting from the right place. We do not say, 'This is a piece of work by a great writer which must be respected as a specimen of the best use of language.' The consideration is rather, 'Knowing what we do about language in general, and about the state of this particular speech-community at the time when this work was written, we are in a position to make an informed judgement.'

There is of course no reason for excluding literary texts from any linguistic investigation or for refusing to treat them exactly the same was as other *paroles*, although some linguists would regard literary language as too deviant to yield much useful information. Linguistically, the literary style can be described without offering any view about its merit, just as legal style can be described without raising questions of justice or liturgical style without raising questions of belief. However, a special interest in any style usually implies some commitment to the intrinsic importance of that which is spoken or written in that style.

One other matter is worth remembering while we still have historical considerations in mind. Linguistic theory, and interest in the nature of language, is not an invention of the twentieth century. Close attention was given to Classical Greek, Latin and Sanskrit by grammarians to whom they were living languages, and nearly every age has produced some views about how language works or should be made to work. The revolution in lingusitics that has taken place in our own time is comparable to the Einsteinian revolution in physics. It has had the similar result of discrediting a great deal of what was formerly believed and making it impossible for intelligent use to be made of the old approach as a basis for investigation.

There are, nevertheless, reasons for giving some attention to the history of linguistic theory and for not closing the mind to all that has gone before. Literature was written by men whose view of language was that of their own age. This is not to say that all imaginative writers were deeply concerned with linguistic theory or spent much time in earnest colloquy with contemporary grammarians. Yet no-one who uses an artistic medium can remain totally unaware of the way in which that medium operates in the community as a whole. One specific point is that the majority of English writers before the latter part of the nineteenth century were educated mainly through the study of Latin, by schoolmasters to whom it was axiomatic that English could and should be described in Latin-based grammatical terms.

Also, and this is a worthy discipline for all whose study requires historical perspective, the fact that any theory can no longer be accepted totally does not mean either that its originators were fools or that it contained nothing fit to be remembered. Literature can still be illuminated by the judgements of those to whom it was fresh, the latest expression of imagination through language. One of the greatest mistakes that can be made is to regard the past as homogeneous. It is easy to laugh at Lord Monboddo in the eighteenth century calling Gothic 'the parent of all the different dialects of the Teutonic'. Yet everyone today must honour the wisdom of John Wallis in 1653 complaining that grammarians had previously 'forced our tongue too much into the pattern of Latin'.

Everyone—well, almost everyone. There are still teachers of English whose consciences should be touched by the words of Wallis. If they venture the Player's excuse, 'I hope we have reformed that indifferently with us', they can be met with Hamlet's admonition, 'Reform it altogether'. Not all the wisdom of the past has been universally recognized. Not all the attitudes of the past need be eschewed by those who have the wisdom of the present. There are ideas which can be lifted out of their shaky framework and fitted into the new. Abuses should never make us disregard right uses.

FURTHER READING

Historical linguistics can be studied in W. P. Lehmann, *Historical Linguistics: an Introduction* (New York, 1962, Holt, Rinehart and Winston), or, in the framework of Chomskyan linguistics in, R. D. King, *Historical Linguistics and Generative Grammar* (Englewood Cliffs, N. J., 1969, Prentice-Hall).

The development of English is surveyed in G. L. Brook, *A History of the English Language* (London, 1958, André Deutsch), which includes an extensive bibliography; aspects particularly relevant to the present study are examined in W. F. Bolton, *A Short History of Literary English* (2nd edn., London, 1967, Edward Arnold). H. C. Wyld, *Historical Study of the Mother Tongue* (London, 1906, John Murray) is an old but not obsolete application of philology to the diachronic study of English.

Good shorter studies are: K. D. Uitti, 'Philology: Factualism and

History' (*Chatman: Style*, pp. 111-32); A. Rodway, 'By Algebra to Augustanism' (*Fowler*, pp. 53-8); J. Norton-Smith, 'Chaucer's Epistolary Style' (*Fowler*, pp. 157-65); R. F. Lawrence, 'The Formulaic Theory and its Application to English Alliterative Poetry' (*Fowler*, pp. 166-83); M. W. Croll, 'The Baroque Style in Prose' (*Chatman: Essays*, pp. 341-61); J. Miles, 'Eras in English Poetry' (*Chatman: Essays*, pp. 175-96).

The history of ideas about language—which is not the same thing as historical linguistics—is covered by R. H. Robins, *A Short History of Linguistics* (London, 1967, Longman).

4
Speech and Writing

Tennyson has left us a brief word picture of how his *Morte d'Arthur* was read aloud:

> The poet little urged,
> But with some prelude of disparagement,
> Read, mouthing out his hollow oes and aes,
> Deep-chested music . . .

Tennyson was not the first major poet to be aware of the distinctive features in his own or other voices, but he was the first whose voice was recorded. It is still possible to hear the old gramophone record, too faint and technically poor to give much idea of the living reality, but yet a link between two eras in the study of language. The development of efficient means of recording the human voice was contemporary with the recognition of speech as the primary mode of language, both as a matter of chronological development and in its importance as a corpus of performance. The portable tape-recorder makes it possible to assemble synchronic evidence before change invalidates it.

With the application of phonetic methods to the spoken utterance, we are no longer satisfied with such verbal descriptions of speech as 'hollow oes and aes'. It would not be true to say that the majority of linguists regard all written language as unimportant or deviant—though the feeling is not unknown—but certainly *language* no longer means chiefly *written language* as it did for the classical philologists. Writing cannot be esteemed as it was when no other record of usage, past or present, was available. The student of literature, still dependent on written texts, may once more seem to be working against the mainstream of linguists. If certain readjustments can be made, however, the result is beneficial to both disciplines.

In the first place, it is unwise to exaggerate the distance between speech and writing in a society like our own where so many people can switch between the two media with little or no effort. The same ease has been felt by the more literate—from whom the makers and readers of literature were mainly drawn—within post-Renaissance European culture. The present day, more perhaps than any previous age, yields examples of borderline usage with features characteristic of one realization emerging in the other. Broadcasting has produced formalized speech to be read aloud from a script, a development of the old more limited skill of 'recitation' or the kind of literary reading aloud that Tennyson described. Conversely, familiar letters incorporate spoken features such as contracted verbal forms and lexical items generally regarded as part of the colloquial register.

We can speak a text or write down a conversation, but in doing either we are reminded of the differences of media. The apparatus of speech consists of bodily organs for articulating and receiving, with sound-waves for transmission. The apparatus of writing consists of visible marks, made by various implements on various types of surface, transmitted by light-waves and received by the eye. Thus we may be led to consider acoustics and physiology on the one hand, typography and optics on the other. It might seem as if there were two different 'languages' to be studied.

What we in fact encounter are the two ways of realizing any given *langue*, the one phonological and the other graphological. They both depend on the same available grammar and lexicon, but the selection made therefrom may be affected by the type of realization. In any stylistic study it is necessary to maintain sensitivity to the influence of the alternative realization which is not actually being examined. Literary language, almost entirely written, will not be appreciated in depth if we stop thinking about speech altogether.

It demands little specialist skill to see the more apparent differences between spoken and written realizations, quite apart from the physical media used. Writing is generally accepted as more 'careful' than speech. Many people feel that they are putting themselves on more permanent record when they write; they are more cautious both about what they say and about how they say it. Consciousness of 'grammar' as a set of prescriptive rules becomes more marked. Even in ephemeral modes such as personal letters, most of us would at least try to divide our discourse into sentences conforming to the old—and imperfect—rule of 'making complete sense and containing at least one finite verb'. A covertly introduced tape-recorder, however, reveals that even the most careful conversation or spoken discussion is full of short phrases, incomplete nominal groups and anacolutha. Thus the adoption of a given register will not always present the same choice and distribution of features. Any user may alter his performance towards a recipient when the occasion changes from conversation to letter-writing.

Such differences as these are not irrational or over-cautious. Written realizations do need better organization than spoken ones, by the very nature of the situation in which they are received. Written texts are normally read by one person silently and alone; speech is normally shared, punctuated by spoken response from one or more other people. The limits are not inviolable: a text may be read aloud and commented upon by those present; a lecture, still more a broadcast talk, will be heard by a number of people but is not likely to evoke spoken response during its course. Nevertheless, the written text may in general be said to demand more skill and more planning. If it is to fulfil its purpose, it must embody a 'message' which has been thought out before transmission and to which the whole text contributes. Spoken realization is usually within a developing situation: written realization must create its own situation. No considerations of discipline or politeness can detain the reader who is bored and whose attention wanders. Nor can any correction or restatement be made in the course of communication.

It may be remarked here that drama is of special interest among the literary kinds for its connection with both types of realization. It is contained—usually, not invariably—in a written text designed to be spoken aloud by different voices, in the presence of auditors. It is planned and presented as a whole work, whose course is determined before transmission begins yet which simulates a developing situation with some element of suspense about the outcome. There is great linguistic as well as theatrical interest in such features as contrived or spontaneous audience participation, improvization on a plot outline and the direct address (whether Elizabethan or Brechtian) to those present at a performance.

Drama of course uses visual as well as spoken means of creating its effect. This fact may remind us that speech is not simply composed of phonemes, or writing of letters. The suprasegmental features of speech such as stress and intonation, embodied in *langue*, are variable according to the habits of the individual performer and the changing demands of the situation. Even paralinguistic features like gesture and facial expression can have communicative value and need to be assessed as part of the whole.

In place of these, written realization has recourse to punctuation, paragraphing, and the blank spaces which may correspond to silence. There is also the multitude of graphological devices such as capitalizing, italics, different founts of type. Literary creation uses prosody, scene-division, chapter units and all the other technical aids which are well known to literary criticism. It is not difficult to see why written texts, and supremely literary texts, were traditionally regarded as the superior form of language and the source of 'rules' for everyday users. They were stable, accessible, carefully planned by those who strove to use language to the best effect.

Yet anyone who aspires to the stylistic study of literature needs to be informed about the spoken features of the *langue* from which his texts are derived. Indeed, any student of literature is missing something if he is entirely ignorant of what modern linguistics has to tell him about phonetics and phonology. Equally, the linguist should not suppose that literature is irrelevant to this aspect of his concern. For the remainder of this chapter, let us consider the main reasons for these assertions.

The first reason is so simple that it is easily ignored. Every writer is a member of a speech-community; the language that he uses came to him in infancy, acquired by a process—still not fully explained today—which was shared with less articulate contemporaries. It needs perhaps some conflict of prestige between languages for the deep personal value of the native tongue to be appreciated. Milton understood the primacy of speech when he turned from Latin to English verse:

> Hail, native language, that by sinews weak
> Didst move my first endeavouring tongue to speak,
> And mad'st imperfect words with childish trips,
> Half unpronounced, slide through my infant lips,
> Driving dumb silence from the portal door,
> Where he had mutely sat two years before.
>
> ('At a Vacation Exercise')

We have seen how a certain dialect may acquire prestige and become the standard for a national literature. It should be remembered that the spoken dialect comes first—and continues to be used for spoken realization even after it has gained other and wider distribution.

The literary writer, however great his achievement, similarly remains a human being who must understand the speech of others and communicate his own needs through speaking. Whether he speaks or writes, and however influenced by the demands of either realization, he must select the items available to him in the *langue* of his speech-community. The common core of that community must direct a great deal of his selection, if there is to be any communication at all. It is from that common core that his usage may be adjudged deviant, with whatever overtones of praise or blame that may be allowed to the critical sense after the linguistic investigation has produced its findings.

Secondly, it is essential to understand that many of those features which are considered to be distinctively 'literary' are phonological and not graphological. Much of the useful work in stylistics, including some of the approaches which will be suggested later in this book, depends on acceptance of this fact. Graphological forms convey these features to our vision, but they act only as substitutes for the auditory effect. A few may be considered briefly at this stage; their critical importance in performance will appear later.

Stress is clearly a function of speech. Without awareness of its 'normal' or everyday occurrence in speech, we should not be able to scan a line of English poetry in the traditional metres or feel the less apparent rhythm of free verse and patterned prose. Syllabic stress operates the distinction between *protest* as a noun and *protest* as a verb; word-stress in spoken sentences allows the shift of implicative emphasis to almost any item which is to be brought into prominence and contrasted with other items. In most varieties of spoken English it is inseparably linked with intonation.

What all this means for the study of prosodic effect in detail will be considered later. The essential point is that the controlled patterning used in many literary kinds owes its effect to our acquaintance with speech. It is true that visual devices can be effective, but mainly as a contribution to auditory perception. Graphology can assist the presentation of dialogue:

'Oh come on then, all the LOT of you', cried Uncle Jim.
(H. G. Wells, *History of Mr. Polly*)

or of non-lingual sounds like the bursting of a shell that breaks the soldier's reverie:

> I'll soon be 'ome. You mustn't fret.
> My feet's improvin', as I told you of.
> We're out in rest now. Never fear.
> (VRACH! By crumbs, but that was near.)
> >   (Wilfred Owen, 'The Letter')

These devices, linked to sound, seem more natural and acceptable than the purely visual shaping of lines to correspond with theme as in Herbert's 'Easter Wings', which is mannered rather than effective. A reader may indeed find something worthwhile in the careful use of line-arrangement and spacing by some free-verse poets, or even the shapes of 'concrete poetry', but these at present are outside the mainstream of literature. Visual shaping is perhaps most effective in comic verse like Carroll's similitude of a mouse's tail in 'Fury said to a mouse'.

The relationship to speech is even more apparent in the use of rhyme, a device which is phonic both in the choosing and the response. Whereas *make* and *break* or *soul* and *scroll* are 'good' rhymes, the dismissive and self-contradictory term 'eye-rhyme' is applied to pairs like *wash* and *dash*. In cases where pronunciation has changed and is not reflected in the spelling, the judgement of rhyme depends on what is heard and not on what is seen unless we can apply some knowledge of historical phonology. Modern poets often prefer the 'chiming' effect of half-rhyme, which rests on the likeness of certain sounds and is even more removed from spelling; it may effectively combine with full rhyme:

> I have met them at close of day
> Coming with vivid faces
> From counter or desk among grey
> Eighteenth-century houses.
> >   (W. B. Yeats, 'Easter 1916')

Rhyme depends on a certain tension between the possibility of its occurrence in the *langue* and its infrequency in the majority of *paroles*. It becomes impossible as a literary device in a language like Japanese in which unintended 'rhymes' are continually occurring in everyday speech.

A third connection between literary and spoken language lies in the echoic or onomatopoeic effect of certain words. The conscious imitation of natural sounds such as *bow-wow* and *cock-a-doodle-do* is familiar to all, particularly in the childish register, and is interesting linguistically for the differences of realization in different languages:

French cocks crow *cocorico*, German ones *kikeriki*, Swedish *kukuliku*. More subtle is the associative effect of certain English consonant clusters such as the quick movement suggested by /fl/ in *fly, flee, flash, flick, fling, flit*; or the hard breaking of /kr/ in *crash, crack, crush, crunch, crumble*.

There is a great deal of work still to be done on the effect of sound-combinations. A careful reader will consider how much appreciation may be owed to phonic effects that are not contained in such formal patterning as rhyme, assonance or alliteration. Phonology can extend into the area of meaning, even though it is not itself referential. The names of some of Dickens's characters, for instance, evoke the type of person who is depicted through more extended verbal description. Sometimes a referential element is present and is enhanced by the whole pattern, as Gradgrind, Bounderby, Snagsby, Smallweed. Elsewhere the effect is associative and largely unconscious: Squeers, Quilp, Pardiggle, Noggs. The name Twemlow fits the man's vagueness and adaptability, re-inforcing Dickens's animistic image of him as a table extended by extra leaves with a suggestion of 'tremble' or 'tremulous' said with a lisp and trailing off into 'low'. Jaggers connects with the jabbing fore-finger, the jagged cragginess of the man both physically and by nature.

A different effect, and one more easily referred to particular phonemes, can be found in the evocation of peaceful rest by the patterning of /s/ and /l/ in poetry:

> Music that gentlier on the spirit lies
> Than tired eyelids upon tired eyes
>> (Tennyson, 'The Lotus Eaters')

> Silence and sleep like fields of amaranth lie
>> (De la Mare, 'All that's past')

A very elementary knowledge of phonetics enables us to note the sibilance of /s/ and /z/, together with the more relaxed articulation of the voiced sound, as if the voiceless beginning of *spirit* drowses off into the voiced endings of *lies, eyelids, eyes*; or *silence* and *sleep* relax into *fields*. At the same time, the liquid /l/ adds to the impression of softness and relaxation and dances with the fricatives so that music—gent*l*ier and *s*pirit—*l*ies leads on to eye*l*id*s* with *l*ies as the hinge where the reversal takes place; so also *s*i*l*ence and *sl*eep yield to the mirror-image of sounds in fie*l*d*s*. In addition, there is strong sound-association to enhance the referential meaning of the words actually used: *slumber, sloth, lassitude, listless, solitude, leisure,* all come to mind.

One more brief example must suffice, with the hope of guiding the reader on his way. Hamlet's indictment of Claudius approaches its climax with lines that sound as if they were spat out of a mouth tense with fury:

> A cutpurse of the empire and the rule,
> That from a shelf the precious diadem stole,
> And put it in his pocket.
>
> (III.iv)

The plosives and harsh consonant clusters are grouped mostly around short close or half-close vowels in a way that suggests the physiological results of inner tension. Through the whole utterance, the /p/ sound recurs with a contemptuous blowing of the lips that eventually underlines the sneer of the colloquial sneak-thief phrase 'put it in his pocket'. The fact that our great poets knew nothing of phonetic theory and that we do is our good fortune, not their insufficiency. They seem to have known by their own ears what we can more deeply appreciate by analysing scientifically. Pope needed no phonetics to understand that

> 'Tis not enough no harshness gives offence:
> The sound must seem an echo to the sense.
>
> (*Essay on Criticism*)

The fourth connection between graphology and phonology is the frequent need to express speech by a literary character. The linguist might well think it an ideal if all dialogue in novels and plays were set down in phonetic script, but this of course would cut off appreciation from the majority of readers; the contrast with the conventional orthography of narrative would certainly produce an original and interesting visual patterning. In practice our writers have had to do their best with the inadequacies of the alphabet, so that we must try imaginatively to interpret the rendering of dialect or idiophonic speech. Shakespeare thus shows Edgar's simulation of peasant character by using the contemporary conventions of rustic speech on the stage:

> Good gentleman, go your gait and let poor volk pass. And chud ha' been swaggered out of my life, 'twould not ha been zo long as 'tis by a vortnight.
>
> (IV.vi)

Dickens does his best with Sarah Gamp's special brand of cockney:

> We never knows wot's written in each other's hearts; and if we had glass winders there, we'd need to keep the shetters up, some on us, I do assure you!
>
> (*Martin Chuzzlewit*, Ch. 29)

Bernard Shaw, who knew something of phonetics, realized that the speech of a character like Drinkwater in *Captain Brassbound's Conversion* 'cannot be indicated save in . . . imperfect manner, without the aid of a phonetic alphabet'. His attempt to use normal typographical resources was highly ingenious, but stretched them to the point of difficulty for the reader:

> Mawt yeppn to the honestest, best meaning pusson, aw do assure yer, gavner.

A modern poet may go further, encouraged by the wider scope granted to impressionism. The poem 'ygUduh' by E. E. Cummings is, visually, meaningless; it has to be read aloud without regard to one's own normal speech, to make its effect. So treated, it is a powerful evocation of mindless prejudice and illiteracy which regards itself as the height of civilization:

ydoan
yunnuhstan

ydoan o
yunnuhstan dem
yguduh ged

yunnuhstan dem doidee
yguduh ged riduh
ydoan o nudn
LISN bud LISN

dem
gud
am

lidl yelluh bas
tuds weer goin

duhSIVILEYEzum

Whatever this might gain in precision from a phonetic transcript would be lost from the evocative visual effect of distribution, spacing and capitalization. Here graphological and phonological systems work together brilliantly.

Conversation of course does not consist of an even sequence of sounds. The writer generally trusts to the reader's personal competence to interpret the created performance of characters with the correct stresses and intonations. He may, as we have seen, use occasional typographical devices to show special emphasis, but over-indulgence here defeats its purpose. We learn to accept as a matter of literary convention that dialogue is written down in well-formed sentences indicated by punctuation; the broken utterance, pauses, repetitions and anacolutha which pass unnoticed in living encounter would become intolerable on the printed page. They can be accepted only as the idiolect of a particular character like Mr. Jingle and shown in contrast with the 'regularity' of other speakers—a regularity which they would not display in real life.

There is no universal way of presenting speech in literature. It is interesting to compare the different degrees of distancing, inherent in the transference of phonological to graphological realization, which a writer will accept. The most common mode is that of direct speech, set out by quotation marks and purporting to reproduce the exact words used by a character. Reported or indirect speech may be said to recognize the problem by disposing of it and using graphological means to set down a message which is clearly not in the terms of conversation. It would destroy any sense of dramatic dialogue were it used all the time. Juxtaposed with direct speech, however, it can be highly effective. The almost aggressive appearance of a purely graphological realization gives a greater reality to the rest; it can give the sense of spoken memory, of distaste or embarrassment, of detachment:

'But, bishop,' said he, 'did you ever read John Hiram's will?'
The bishop thought probably he had, thirty-five years ago, when first instituted to his see.

(Trollope, *The Warden*)

'Marriages with cousin,' said Mrs. Swithin, 'can't be good for the teeth.'
Bart put his finger inside his mouth and projected the upper row outside his lips. They were false. Yet, he said, the Olivers

D

hadn't married cousins. The Olivers couldn't trace their descent for more than two or three hundred years. But the Swithins could. The Swithins were there before the Conquest.

(Virginia Woolf, *Between the Acts*)

The traditional distinction of direct and indirect speech is not absolute. Ever since Bally coined the description *style indirecte libre* in 1912, critics have noted how features of direct speech can be incorporated, to a greater or lesser degree, in discourse which is ostensibly narrative. Thus Jane Austen, retaining the characteristics already attributed to Miss Bates in direct speech, distances them sufficiently to make them appear as part of Emma's auditory perception rather than as outgoing utterance:

Indeed the truth was, that poor dear Jane could not bear to see anybody—anybody at all—Mrs. Elton, indeed, could not be denied—and Mrs. Cole had made such a point—and Mrs. Perry had said so much—but, except them, Jane would really see nobody.

(*Emma*, Ch. 45)

Bolder experiments have been made by writers who try to get inside the mind of a character, to record the largely uncontrolled sequence of thought through verbalization. The nexus of sense-impressions from without and response from within takes us beyond the communicative level of language, yet not to a state where we can say that language ceases to operate. Joyce thus begins the 'Sirens' section of *Ulysses* as Leopold Bloom's present consciousness and past memories encounter the sights and sounds of a city bar at lunchtime:

Bronze by gold heard the hoofirons, steelyringing
Imperthnthn thnthnthn.
Chips, picking chips off rocky thumbnail, chips.
Horrid! And gold flushed more.
A husky fifenote blew.
Blew. Blue bloom is on the
Gold pinnacled hair.
A jumping rose on satiny breasts of satin, rose of Castille.
Trilling, trilling: Idolores.

Here the graphological realization strains beyond its accepted limits to accommodate speech, thought and music. Perhaps Pater had a point for stylistics when he said that all art constantly aspires towards the condition of music.

FURTHER READING

Readers to whom modern theories of speech are new should start with J. D. O'Connor, *Phonetics* (Harmondsworth, 1971, Penguin Books). The best recent application of phonetics to present-day English is A. C. Gimson, *An Introduction to the Pronunciation of English* (2nd edn., London, 1970, Edward Arnold).

The relationship between poetry and speech is studied by F. Berry, *Poetry and the Physical Voice* (London, 1963, Routledge and Kegan Paul); see also K. M. Wilson, *Sound and Meaning in English Poetry* (London, 1930, Jonathan Cape).

The effects on rhyme of phonological change are the subject of H. C. Wyld, *Studies in English Rhymes from Surrey to Pope* (London, 1923, John Murray).

Important shorter studies include: D. I. Masson, 'Vowel and Consonant Patterns in Poetry' (*Chatman: Essays*, pp. 3-18); D. Hymes, 'Phonological Aspects of Style: some English Sonnets' (*Chatman: Essays*, pp. 33-53); I. Fónagy, 'The Functions of Vocal Style' (*Chatman: Style*, pp. 159-76); also *Leech*, pp. 89-100.

Attention is given to this aspect of the work of particular authors in R. Quirk, *Charles Dickens and Appropriate Language* (Durham, 1959, Durham University Press); W. J. Bate, *The Stylistic Development of Keats* (London, 1958, Routledge and Kegan Paul). W. K. Wimsatt, *The Verbal Icon* (Kentucky, 1954, Kentucky University Press), studies the rhymes of Alexander Pope, pp. 157-64.

5
Syntax

The traditional debate about 'poetic diction' turned mainly on the poet's choice of words. The concern of modern linguistics, however, has been increasingly with syntax: an emphasis by which literary stylistics is by no means the loser. Word-selection can be seen in a wider perspective of language which deepens former insights as well as offering new ones. It should not be difficult to agree with F. S. Scott's view that 'A writer's style is often expressed as much by the grammatical clauses and structures he prefers as by his choice oi words' (*English Grammar*).

A few general observations may be useful at this point; the reader who already has a fair knowledge of linguistics is asked to excuse both their intrusion and their oversimplified form. Their importance to the total discussion will not be confined to syntax alone.

There are two distinct ways in which the relationships between words may be understood. In any sentence, the words composing it stand in a *syntagmatic* relationship by their order and placing. It is a linear connection, as can be seen in the graphological realization of a sentence on the page. It is, in fact, the kind of sequence which anyone who was not concerned with linguistic terminology might refer to as 'grammatical' or as 'forming a sentence'. There is a syntagmatic relationship which allows us to be satisfied, as native speakers, with such everyday sentences as:

> I shall see him next week.
> The milk is on the doorstep.

These are examples of words, or more properly *signs*, placed in a relative order which seems to be 'correct' for present-day English. The reason for its being correct can be stated in different ways according to the grammar of the language that we decide to use. Note that there are many usable grammars, both actual and potential:

correctness does not depend on the ability to be explained in the traditional Latin-based grammar. Note too that the *syntagmatic* progression is theoretically unlimited and in practice is often considerably extended. There is no formal limit to the length of a sentence.

Words can be related in another way, which is known as *paradigmatic*. A word used in an actual *parole* stands in relation to many other words in the *langue* which have not been chosen on this occasion. They are available for use in the same syntagmatic manner as the word which has in fact been used: they share the same syntagmatic possibilities. Thus in the first sentence used as illustration above, *I* is in paradigmatic relationship with *you*, *he*, *she*, *we* . . . that is, with all the words generally known as 'personal pronouns'. The word *see* relates with a much larger number of possible words, transitive verbs like *tell*, *hear*, *answer*, *disappoint*, *please*, *kick*. . . . In the second sentence, the space occupied by *milk* could accommodate an even larger number of nouns—*bread*, *paper*, *dog*, *visitor*, *mat*, *parcel*. . . . It will be clear that we are not at present concerned with meaning, only with what is possible within the pattern.

A native speaker makes these relationships without much effort or conscious thought for most of his linguistic communication. Linguists, however, like to have a grammar; and a grammar is satisfactory if it can produce all the sentences that would be acceptable to the native speaker, and no other sentences. Obviously it does not have to attempt the impossible task of formulating every sentence that could be uttered, but it must be able to meet the challenge offered by any acceptable sentence that appears. In the past, one type of grammar became prescriptive so that sentences were tested by it and grammarians tended to forget that it was just as important to keep testing the grammar by the sentences. If a sentence cannot be generated by the grammar and yet is unquestionably acceptable, the grammar needs some modification. It is not satisfactory to take refuge in talking about 'exceptions to the rule'.

Now a sentence may, conversely, fit the grammar and yet be unacceptable; or, more often, there may be argument about whether it is acceptable or not. This is where we need to ask the questions proper to stylistics, and in particular to literary stylistics. Such a situation is caused by a *deviant* sentence. We have looked briefly at the question of deviation—of sentences well-formed grammatically but not semantically. The whole notion of deviation in literary language is most important and should be accepted without presuppositions about the quality of such language, though it may help a new approach to qualitative questions. Nor is deviation only concerned with syntax; it can be phonic, as when a poet chooses to make *wind* have the sound /waind/ to rhyme with *behind* as Shelley does in the 'Ode to the West Wind'. It can also—and this we shall see later—be paradigmatic.

Even in syntax, deviation is not precisely defined, although few people would nowadays be prepared to stigmatize every disputable sentence as 'ungrammatical'. That which is not grammatically well-formed can be easily recognized through any workable grammar, which must reject such sentences as **The men is here* or **It was John what done it*. (The asterisk is used to denote an unacceptable realization.) This kind of performance makes us suspect inadequate competence, although account must be taken of both dialect and idiolect. For instance, the second of these examples would be accepted in a familiar spoken register by a large number of English people.

Deviation need not be ungrammatical or contrary to any rules. It may result from taking fuller than normal advantage of the possibilities open to every user. There is a kind of deviation which simply exploits the fact that a syntagmatic progression has no upper limit. There is no rule about the maximum number of co-ordinating clauses which can follow one another: a long progression of 'ands' is usually regarded as clumsy, but it is justly admired when Shakespeare uses it in his sixty-sixth Sonnet for an extended indictment of the ills attendant on contemporary life. Nor is there any limit to the number of adjectives which can precede and modify a noun, though prescriptive manuals of 'good style' have tended, rightly, to advise against too many qualifiers. But Swinburne took advantage of the freedom, adding to it the phonic link of internal rhyme with the verse:

> Villion, our sad, bad, glad, mad brother's name.

Granted then the open-ended nature of language, deviation is not always easy to pick out. Within the limits of grammatical acceptability, one native speaker may form without question a sentence which seems deviant to another. We must agree with Chomsky that speakers continually generate and recognize unique sentences. The grammar and lexicon together give all that is needed for an infinite extension of understanding. It is unlikely that anyone has previously formulated the following sentence in English:

My aunt's mauve hockey-stick was made by an albino in Runcorn.

Any native speaker must agree that this sentence is both grammatically and semantically well-formed. Any oddity which it suggests is due to the nature of the supposed and as yet unverified reference, not to anything deviant in the syntagmatic or paradigmatic pattern. This kind of oddity is more likely to be met in literature than in other styles: its quality will depend on its relationship to larger units than the sentence. The creative writer has hope for a general recognition of the validity of sentences that are both new and unexpected, for this is the basis of his communication. To adapt an Orwellian phrase, all users generate unique sentences but some users' sentences are more unique than others.

The grammar limits our freedom but seldom troubles us. The syntagmatic relationships which we acquire in the process of learning to use the mother tongue do not interfere with the message unless there is some startling departure from what is expected. Yet these relationships are of prime importance for even the most trivial communication. They control the presentation of ideas, their order and consequently their connection and continuity. The syntax is a familiar and comforting framework for assured communication. Without being aware of the fact, we are continually glancing ahead in the course of a conversation, enabled to anticipate what is likely to come by reason of what has gone. Each step in a syntagmatic line allows certain possibilities of continuation and rejects others. Unconscious familiarity allows us to break in and answer an unfinished utterance in the mother tongue, whereas it would be necessary to wait and hear the total message in a foreign language in which competence was imperfect.

To revert for easy example to the sentence *The milk is on the doorstep*: by the time we have reached *The milk is* . . . the possibilities of syntagmatic progression are still large and varied. The addition of the single item *on* at once closes the possibility of words like *sour, boiling, ready, dear* . . . but leaves the possibility of *time, order, demand,* which in turn disappear with the addition of *the* to the sequence. Thus choice is progressively restricted, within a set of rules which already exclude certain other possibilities. We are precluded from **Milk the is on doorstep the,* and even *On the doorstep the milk is* seems to be extremely doubtful and at best dialectal. Yet there is freedom in the ordering of certain sequences: *On the doorstep is the milk* is odd but not ungrammatical, while *Tomorrow I shall see him* is neither ungrammatical nor odd, though it may be recognized as giving a different prominence within the sentence.

Although English has a rigid word-order in some respects, as the result of the disappearance of morphological indications of grammatical relationship, it allows freedom which the native user learns to handle for emphasis. We should feel no hesitation in either uttering or accepting the emotional overtones in so simple an inversion as *Over went the chair* instead of *The chair went over*. The writer of literature has access to these possibilities in whatever register he is working. We hear the authoritarian tone of Lady Bracknell in

Songs in French I cannot allow

and we are moved by the emotional stress of Keats's 'Tender is the night' or recognize the dynamic inversion of narrative verb, subject and qualifier, contrasted with the normative order of speech in Macaulay's

Then out spake Spurius Lartius;
A Ramnian proud was he:
'Lo, I will stand at thy right hand,
And keep the bridge with thee.'

This discussion introduces another concept that is important in stylistics, illustrated but by no means exhausted by the possibility of inversion, and not confined to syntax. The word *foregrounding* is used to describe the kind of deviation which has the function of bringing some item into artistic emphasis so that it stands out from its surroundings. It is helpfully described by M. A. K. Halliday as 'prominence that is motivated'. The notion is owed to the Prague School of linguistics and the English word was first suggested by P. L. Garvin as a rendering of the Czech *aktualisce*. Foregrounding may be recognized in other arts as well as literature and is particularly important in the composition of a painting.

With these concepts in mind, we can look at some of the questions which arise in the syntax of literature, remembering that any linguistic utterance involves some tension between the rules on which communication depends and the freedom which the user's unique situation demands. The deeper the artistic concern with the manner as well as the matter, the greater the tension is likely to become. In everyday discourse, syntax and message co-operate without troubling anyone very much. In literature—and perhaps in some other styles with distinctive features—syntax becomes more conscious and is likely to make the user intolerant of its restrictions. It is in this area that the difference between literary and colloquial performance is seen most clearly.

In one sense, literary language has the greater freedom. Just as it has been suggested that no register can be excluded from the total concern of literature, so no choice of generation from the grammar is forbidden. Other styles may constrict or enjoin: recipes and instruction manuals make considerable use of the imperative, which is seldom found in pure science or literary criticism. Liturgy and preaching show a particular need for the shared imperative, 'Let us. . . '. The style of Parliamentary debate forbids the use of the second person in referring to other members. Literary fashions and the pressures of critics may indeed limit the writer if he chooses to heed them, but literature itself acknowledges no prohibitions.

Yet there are pressures from the grammar itself, and it is these which may result in deviation. Any writer must use, except with deliberate archaism, the syntax available in his own time. In some ways we may think that English syntax has lost a certain amount of strength over the centuries. The present-day writer is forbidden the emphasis of repeated negatives that was open to Chaucer:

> He never yet no vileyne ne sayde
> In al his lyf, unto no manner wight
> *(General Prologue)*

and the doubled superlative of Shakespeare's

> This was the most unkindest cut of all
> *(Julius Ceasar, III.ii)*

Poets may feel the later language to be overloaded with prepositional phrases and post-modifying clauses and long for the freedom of ellipsis leading to the compressed pre-modification of Old English:

> Hi leton þa of folman feolhearde speru
> grimme gegrundene fleogan
> *(Battle of Maldon)*

(Literally: 'They let then from fists file-hard spears, grimly-ground darts fly').

Some indeed are not content to long for it: they claim it:

> Tom—garlanded with squat and surly steel
> Tom; then Tom's fallowbootfellow piles pick
> By him and rips out rockfire homeforth—sturdy Dick.
> > (Hopkins, 'Tom's Garland')

> It is spring, moonless night in the small town, starless and bible-black, the cobblestreets silent and the hunched courters'-and-rabbits' wood limping invisible down to the sloeblack, slow, black, crowblack, fishingboat-bobbing sea.
> > (Dylan Thomas, *Under Milk Wood*)

Such deviation is not alien to the syntax, rather inherent in the historical development and open to the writer who wishes to range along the diachronic as well as the synchronic axis.

These liberties with syntax involve experiments in *morphology*—the actual forms of the words used in the pattern. Morphological deviation does not play a great part in literature while the normal syntagmatic relationships are being observed and is not generally of great stylistic interest. It may appear in a period of experiment and uncertainty about the limits of the *langue*, as in the sixteenth century in this country when a good deal of free movement was permitted between word-classes. Shakespeare's audience was probably less startled than a modern one by such lines as

> Come, brother John, full bravely hast thou fleshed
> Thy maiden sword.
> > (*1 Henry IV*, V.iv)

> Why should you fall into so deep an O?
> > (*Romeo and Juliet*, III.iii)

The rearrangement of morphemes as a humorous device is acceptable even in the less flexible state of the present-day language and is readily comprehended. There is, for instance, the schoolboy's mnemonic:

> Kalends come upon the oneth,
> Nones the fifth day of the month

or the liberties taken by Ogden Nash, such as:

Let us pause to consider the English,
Who when they pause to consider themselves they get all
                         reticently thrilled and tinglish.

Morphological deviation is open to more serious writers who are exploring the boundaries of language, as Hopkins with 'goldengrove unleaving' or Joyce with 'Liffeying waters of, hither and thithering waters of, Night' and 'eagerquietly'.

There is some interest in the study of single features in a writer's syntax, but any convincing conclusion depends on the pursuit of the feature over a wider range of his work than is possible here. The reader is referred to the reading-list at the end of this chapter. For our present purpose, however, it is wise to confine attention to the manipulation of syntax within a small section of a text.

Mention has been made of foregrounding through deviation from normal word-order. Here are two more examples, the first giving prominence to epithets not startling in themselves and leading to the normal word-order of a simile which achieves its emphasis as a figure of rhetoric containing a repeated epithet, without recourse to syntactic deviation:

> Maiden still the morn is; and strange she is, and secret;
> Strange her eyes; her cheeks are cold as cold sea-shells.
>   (George Meredith, *Love in the Valley*)

In the second, the feminine pronoun is placed after its verb and gives a sense of action that is involuntary, unmotivated by the doer, leading to the restoration of the pronoun to its dominant position when the narrator enters a joint action:

> Thus leant she and lingered—joy and fear!
> Thus lay she a moment on my breast.
> Then we began to ride.
>   (Robert Browning, *The Last Ride Together*)

Syntactic rules do not account for the ordering of words from a common class, and here the considerations are purely stylistic. The choice is, nevertheless, often important and occurs within the syntagmatic progression. There is no syntactic rule by which to judge the position of *Bibles* in the series of nouns which make up Pope's description of Belinda's dressing-table, yet no other placing would fulfil the irony of the juxtaposition so well:

> Puffs, powders, patches, Bibles, billet-doux
>
> (*The Rape of the Lock*, Canto I)

Here of course the question of metrical placing also enters; this consideration does not affect the ordering of the verbs by Sidney:

> Virtue awake, beauty but beauty is:
> I may, I must, I can, I will, I do
> Leave following that which it is gain to miss,
> Let her go: soft, but there she comes . . .

Here the sequence is determined by the imagined thought-process that leads from subjunctive to indicative governing of the key verb *leave*. A better-known example, of particular interest, is in Ophelia's lament over Hamlet's supposed madness:

> O what a noble mind is here o'erthrown!
> The courtier's, soldier's scholar's, eye, tongue, sword.

Here the sense of derangement is heightened by the fact that the order of the genitive nouns does not correspond semantically with the order of the things possessed. But there is syntactic deviation too in the separation of each possessor from its possessed, so that both logic and the normal expectations of speech seem confounded in the disaster.

Deliberate repetition of a single item has been noticed. The effect is even more striking when repetition takes place in a longer syntagmatic sequence: as we have seen, each successive item is likely to narrow the possible choices for what is to follow, and the writer can work on our expectation by his skill in taking what paths are open to him. Here is a passage from *Hard Times* in which Dickens uses the device in order to heighten his attack on the callousness of the Coketown millowners.

> They were ruined, when they were required to send labouring children to school; they were ruined, when inspectors were appointed to look into their works; they were ruined, when such inspectors considered it doubtful whether they were quite justified in chopping people up with their machinery; they were utterly undone, when it was hinted that perhaps they need not always make quite so much smoke.

Three times the sequence, 'They were ruined, when . . . ' opens the possibility of a temporal-conditional clause, and each time the emphasis of the repetition is countered by the quiet, almost apologetic appeal of what follows. Repetition gives ironic foregrounding to the desired reforms, rising to the climax of the even stronger indicative 'they were utterly undone' that drops into the supremely reasonable final clause.

Repetition of syntactic structures need not include the same lexical items. The striking effect of the opening of Mathew Arnold's *The Scholar Gipsy* is achieved by the repetition of imperatives:

> Go, for they call you, Shepherd, from the hill;
> Go, Shepherd, and untie the wattled cotes:
> No longer leave thy wistful flock unfed,
> Nor let thy bawling fellows rack their throats,
> Nor the cropped grasses shoot another head.
> But when the fields are still,
> And the tired men and dogs all gone to rest,
> And only the white sheep are sometimes seen
> Cross and recross the strips of moon-blanched green;
> Come, Shepherd, and again begin the quest.

The monosyllabic imperative *go* is twice uttered, to be followed by other verbs in the same mood seeming to drift away into the indicative of the linked *when* clauses, only to be sharply drawn back to the parallel but contrasting imperative *come*. The succeeding stanzas change the grammatical mood, as they begin the story of the scholar who rejected all imperatives and went his own way.

Literary syntax may be effective without either deviation or repetition: it is a field as yet little explored, but much would seem to depend on the skill with which the writer manipulates the possibilities so that our expectations of what may follow are fulfilled or defeated. Something depends on the involuntary anticipation of syntagmatic progression. Expectation may be defeated excitingly, but without deviation, when a commonplace pattern leads to a freshly generated conclusion:

> Now that my ladder's gone,
> I must lie down where all the ladders start,
> In the foul-rag-and-bone shop of the heart.
> > (W. B. Yeats, *The Circus Animals' Desertion*)

or one commonplace leads to another not usually found in juxta-position:

> I hope they do give you the Nobel Prize
> it would serve you right
> (William Carlos Williams, 'To my friend Ezra Pound')

But the defeated expectation may be disappointing and banal:

> For months of life has he in store,
> As he to you will tell;
> For still the more he works, the more
> Do his weak ankles swell.
> (Wordsworth, 'Simon Lee')

where the syntactic deviance of the second line is felt to be a cheat, leading to no purpose.

The fulfilled expectation can be exciting too in a certain literary register, where the very 'normality' of the syntax invites close attention to the whole statement instead of foregrounding any item within it. The writer projects a significant image or thought without aggression against the grammar of the language:

> She died in the upstairs bedroom
> By the light of the evening star
> That shone through the plate glass window
> From over Leamington Spa.
> (John Betjeman, 'Death in Leamington')

The fulfilment of expectation, however, can be banal or disastrous if the thought is as predictable or familiar as the syntax which accommodates it, as in Alfred Austin's effusion on the illness of Edward VII:

> Along the line the electric message came,
> 'He is not better, he is much the same',

or William MacGonagall on the Tay Whale:

> I know fishermen in general are often very poor,
> And God in His goodness sent it to drive poverty from their door.

While what seems to be unplanned syntax may be highly effective, that which seems to be deviant may be only compressed, pruned of the structural words in favour of a tighter concentration of form words. It is no new phenomenon, though most frequent in the present century and corresponding to similar structural economies in other arts. It can reproduce the thought-process, imperfectly verbalized:

> Same blue serge dress she had two years ago, the nap bleaching. Seen its best days. Wispish hair over her ears. And that dowdy toque, three old grapes to take the harm out of it. Shabby genteel. She used to be a tasty dresser. Lines round her mouth.
>
> (James Joyce, *Ulysses*)

A question remains: which grammar should be used in judging the syntax of literature? It is advisable to be eclectic in this as in other aspects of literary stylistics, and not to shun the possible insights even of traditional grammar, which was available to most of our writers and through which their own notions about language were formulated. It is impossible, however, to ignore the system developed by Noam Chomsky, who indeed has drawn on some aspects of traditional grammar more closely than did his structuralist predecessors.

It would be neither reasonable nor appropriate to attempt even the briefest introduction to transformational-generative grammar. Readers who are unfamiliar with it have several sources of instruction available to them. There is no reason to suppose that what Chomsky has done is the last word on grammar for all time, but many linguists consider it the best mode of description so far developed. A word on the basic distinction between deep and surface structure may indicate its possible importance to the student of literature.

Other grammars do not account for the sentences which seem to be syntactically identical yet do not produce the same kind of meaning:

> John is eager to please.
> John is easy to please.
>
> I persuaded the doctor to examine him.
> I expected the doctor to examine him.

The apparent identity of these sentences is found only in the *surface structure*—the actual phonological or graphological realization which is presented for inspection. Underlying every actual sentence there will be the *deep structure*—the grammatical structure of the base from which the surface structure is generated in which the semantic meaning of the sentence must be sought. Thus although *John* seems to stand in the same syntagmatic position in each of the first two sentences quoted above, in the deep structure he is shown to be the subject of the first sentence and the object of the second. A similar result comes from analysing what is 'really' being said about *doctor* in each of the second pair of sentences.

Therefore what is violated by an unacceptable sentence such as **The men is here* can be seen to be surface structure; it is at this level that the everyday judgements of grammaticality are made. So also the variations in word-order that have been quoted will affect only the surface structure: they are of course none the less interesting from the point of view of literary syntax. Deep structure is violated by the appearance of an item which is not generally accepted in that particular position in relation to the other items. Deviation of this kind is caused by the italicized words in the following:

> The branches shake down sand along a crawling air,
> and drinks are *miles* towards the sun
> > (Terence Tiller, 'Lecturing to Troops')

> Do not go *gentle* into that good night
> > (Dylan Thomas, 'Do not go gentle')

> Valuing himself not a little upon his elegance, being indeed a proper man of his person, this *talkative* now applied himself to his dress.
> > (James Joyce, *Ulysses*)

All these choices go beyond questions of the startling (like the 'crawling air' of the first quotation) or the unusual (like the deliberate archaism of Joyce's 'a proper man of his person'). They do something which is a liberty not normally permitted in other styles of the present-day language. In terms of syntax they must be called wrong or mistaken selections. Here the literary style shows another of its unique features: the writer masters language below the surface level and claims the right of performance beyond the normal competence. Whether we applaud or disallow the performance depends on judgements which are not those of the linguist. But if we applaud, the insights of the linguist enable us to understand just what it is that we are applauding.

FURTHER READING

Syntax is so great a concern of modern linguistics that the reader who has studied any of the books in the list following Chapter 1 will have made some acquaintance with it. Another useful book, cited on p. 44, is F. S. Scott *et al.*, *English Grammar: a Linguistic Study of its Classes and Structures* (London, 1968, Heinemann); see pp. 213-24 for a survey of the history of English grammar and its current developments.

Applications of grammar to literary criticism are made by D. Davie, *Articulate Energy* (London, 1955, Routledge and Kegan Paul) and F. Berry, *Poet's Grammar* (London, 1958, Routledge and Kegan Paul). Particular studies of single grammatical items of the type mentioned on p. 51 will be found in G. R. Hamilton, *The Tell-tale Article* (London, 1949, Heinemann); L. Spitzer, *Linguistics and Literary History* (Princeton, 1948, Princeton University Press)— see pp. 10-14 for discussion of the use of the phrase *à cause de* by Charles-Louis Phillippe; H. Weinreich, 'The Textual Function of the French Article' (*Chatman: Style*, pp. 221-40).

The syntax of literature is considered by *Leech*, pp. 44-6; *Nowottny*, pp. 187-222 (a detailed examination of a poem by Dylan Thomas); W. N. Francis, 'Syntax and Literary Interpretation' (*Chatman: Essays*, pp. 209-16); S. R. Levin, 'Poetry and Grammaticalness' (*Chatman: Essays*, pp. 224-30); D. Davie, 'Syntax and Music in *Paradise Lost*' in F. Kermode, ed., *The Living Milton* (London, 1960, Routledge and Kegan Paul).

A diachronic survey is made by W. E. Baker, *Syntax in English Poetry 1870-1930* (Berkeley and Los Angeles 1967, California University Press).

On the Prague School and *aktualisce* see P. L. Garvin, *A Prague School Reader on Esthetics, Literary Structure and Style*, (Washington, D.C., 1964, Georgetown University Press).

E

6
Words and Meanings

'What do you read, my lord?'—'Words, words, words.' The exchange between Hamlet and Polonius might be echoed by the literary critic who is asked to state the basic material of his study. It is not, however, an answer that entirely commends itself to the present-day linguist, whose attention is directed more towards syntax and phonology than towards the words which had traditionally seemed the irreducible atomic components of language. It is not that words are no longer held to be important, rather that attempts to think of them as things in themselves, apart from other features of language, raise difficulties.

Even the title of this chapter could be criticized as imprecise, for the definition of *word* is not straightforward. When language is seen primarily as speech, it becomes apparent that words are not neatly segmented as they are by spaces in graphological realization. The pauses in speech do not consistently correspond with word-endings; many languages, including English, do not make it clear to a foreign listener where the utterance is divided into words. Even the written page is full of complications in this respect. Bloomfield made an advance when he defined a word as 'a minimal free form'— the smallest unit of meaning that can exist in isolation, but this does not help us unreservedly. Is *newspaper-seller* a word, or *petrol-station*, or *computer-programmer*? They certainly convey 'bits' of meaning which we do not automatically break into smaller units when we meet them in common use. So too we can make total response to the epithets in Joyce's phrase 'the bullockbefriending bard' or Shakespeare's 'world without end hour', although they do not follow the regular adjective pattern. At the other extreme, we may regard an affix as less than a word. Yet people will speak confidently about 'different isms and ologies', or respond to a sentence like, 'Some were in favour of the idea, but most were very anti', without filing a complaint of deviance.

Again, in an attempt to make a count of all the words in present-day English, how do we assess the set *teach, teaching, teacher, teachable*, to say nothing of the change to *taught*? If a foreigner learns the form *teach* and has some knowledge of methods of word-formation, how many words has he learned? Even more important, how many words has he learned in recognizing as units the sequence of sounds which are written down as *pipe, match, box, balance*? For each of these, and for many other 'words', the dictionary offers a number of apparently different meanings.

These are some of the simpler and more obvious problems—there are many others—which confront those who are trying to deal linguistically with 'words'. It is important to recognize that they exist and not to suppose that words can be treated as isolated linguistic phenomena. The traditional method of language-teaching was concerned with accidence, syntax and vocabulary; and indeed it generally worked well enough in the hands of a good teacher for the practical acquisition of a language. The structuralists though, instead of phonology, grammar and semantics, breaking some of the rigid divisions which prevented deeper understanding of language as a human phenomenon. Chomsky and his followers prefer to discuss grammar as possessing phonological, syntactic and semantic aspects.

All this is of the greatest importance in linguistics and may help our present study—if only because there is still no definitive theory of semantics and it is exciting to follow what is being done in this field. It will not do too much harm, however, if we continue to use the term 'word' and to pursue words in their relationships to one another. Literary writers in all ages have experienced what T. S. Eliot called, 'the intolerable wrestle with words'. Although they may have formulated no linguistic theories, they knew well enough that meaning is not to be sought only at the level of the single word. It is contained in the smaller units as well: in the affixes, and in the inflexions which are few in modern English but were once numerous.

Recognition of meaning within a smaller unit than the word makes it possible to compose new units which will themselves be more readily recognized in their own right. Meaningful neologisms depend on competence which splits the seemingly atomic word and takes from it something that still communicates. However much we may dislike neologisms like *motorcade* or *washeteria*, however much we deplore the etymological inaccuracy of *paratroop*, we cannot deny their semantic function. They take their places in the paradigms of similarly classifiable words, with Shakespeare's *enskyed* and Carroll's *chortle*, and with the less overtly derived coinages like Spenser's *blatant*.

It is, however, meaning that spreads beyond word-boundaries which is of the greatest interest. If we look at the lexicon of any *langue*—the store of words available to its users at a given time—we are presented with countless possibilities of combination. The lexicon is neither infinite nor static in itself. There will always be the hypothesis of phonemic sequences which are derived from the phonology but are inadmissible as words because they convey no agreed meaning, and the lexicon is constantly losing items which become archaic, as well as receiving neologisms. Yet even a lexicon much smaller than that of present-day English offers a seemingly infinite series of syntagmatic and paradigmatic choices. A syntagmatic sequence is correctly realized, appropriate choices from the lexicon are inserted in their places—and we once again marvel at the power of human beings to generate new and unique sentences that are immediately comprehensible. No single user will possess the whole lexicon, and performance does not draw on the whole range even of what is theoretically possessed. Yet a skilful writer has a large potential choice and exercises it widely. His choices are among the matters to be examined through stylistics.

We have perhaps seen enough to be wary of some of the words used in the preceding paragraph. It has become clear that literary writers have a habit of going beyond the conventions of common speech in questions of what is 'correct', which choices are 'appropriate', even what is to be regarded as 'comprehensible', and in other matters. One thing they share with the rest of us, though with different intensity—the tension between freedom and constraint which lies beneath all linguistic performance. For most of us the tension is slightly and rarely felt, as when we are 'feeling for a word', 'at a loss for words', 'trying to put it better'. The degree of tension in literary creation was expressed by T. S. Eliot in *Burnt Norton*:

> Words strain, crack and sometimes break, under the burden,
> Under the tension, slip, slide, perish, Decay with imprecision,
> will not stay in place, Will not stay still.

The freedom of choice becomes anarchic without restriction. We have seen how the rules of syntax operate to reduce the number of possible choices as a sequence progresses; and also that the literary style sometimes defies the prohibition. Syntagmatic deviation is comparatively simple to detect and to judge. Paradigmatic deviation is a different matter, since the choice from the paradigm must be judged with regard to meaning and is therefore less readily referable to the rules. Yet in this relationship too each choice is to some extent restricted by what precedes and restrictive of what follows.

The restrictions may be imposed by external forces, and these need to be recognized in any stylistic approach. The influence of critics—and of creative writers themselves—in the imposition of 'high style' and 'poetic diction' has already been mentioned. It is an influence which belongs to literary history but which cannot be discounted in criticism; and one example must stand for many. In *The Impartial Critick* (1718), John Dennis makes a prescriptive comment on Waller's couplet:

> So Jove from Ida did both hosts survey,
> And when he pleas'd to thunder, part the fray.

'Is not that a noble similitude?' Dennis asks, and answers thus:

> Yes; but the word Fray is altogether unworthy of the greatness of the thought and the dignity of heroic verse. Fray is fitter to express a quarrel between drunken bullies than between the Grecian and Trojan heroes.

This is one kind of basis for a writer's choice, and it is of a kind with the advice given in manuals of good writing, headed by the work of the Fowler brothers, *The King's English*, which is admirable in its own terms.

Formal considerations, too, may condition the choice of words: phonological requirements of rhyme and alliteration, as well as metrical ones. Fashion, form, meaning—and the imponderable personal factor which is most interesting of all—may seem a heavy concentration of armament on one little word. Yet such concentration may be one of the factors which distinguish literature from other linguistic styles. To put it in basic terms, it is because a writer takes such care with his language that we may believe it worthwhile to apply some special technical methods to the result. Criticism which pays regard only to discrete words will not greatly heighten perception or increase response, but any and every critical approach to a work of literature is made through the words which constitute it. The famous Prague Manifesto of 1926, a signpost to the development of literary stylistics, recognized that there is no getting away from the words. George Steiner interprets part of its statement thus:

> The study of a poem is an attempt to register exhaustively the semantic elements or signal structure of which that poem is made and through which, alone, it reaches our consciousness.
>
> (*Minnis*, p. 123)

The use of the phrase 'signal structure' here emphasizes a basic truth about language: words are signs, not things. We all know, of course, that the sounds or letters which make up the word *tree* are not identical with any tangible vegetable growth. The word points our attention, to a particular tree or to a concept formulated from a number of observed trees, without itself partaking of a single characteristic that could be called 'tree-like'. This is clear, except when we react emotively or superstitiously to words as if they somehow *are* the things that they denote, or if we are stupid enough to find something uniquely correct in *tree* and are incredulous that any sensible person would call the same object *arbre* or *baum* or *albero*. The identification of words with things is of some psychological and anthropological interest; it has implications for our present purpose too.

The word *nightingale* is not a small brown bird that sings by night; neither is *rossignol*, *luscinia*, *Philomel*, or *light-winged Dryad of the trees*. Yet all these point to the same creature—the first in what we should call a foreign language, the second in technical zoological description, and the others . . .? We are back with the question of appropriate register, for the last two are clearly 'literary' and acceptable only in a certain kind of context. Each of the four has a place where it seems to fit, isolated from others where it would be awkward or deviant. We adjust our expectations and meet it without surprise, once we have accepted that a particular register is being used.

Now it may be felt that this close consideration of single words is removed from daily speech and listening and is somewhat artificial. The point may readily be conceded; the linguist J. R. Firth held that words operate in social situations where we pay little attention to single items such as would receive separate entries in a glossary. Our response is *holophrastic*, made to a total meaning and not to the sequence of separate meanings. Single words are noted only when they are brought into prominence by being particularly striking, disquieting or shocking. In other words, when they are foregrounded and possibly appear deviant.

The response to a work of literature is properly to the whole text, just as an intelligent response to any linguistic realization must be to the whole. Yet single words impinge on the mind more often in literature than in other styles, and it is part of the writer's art that they should do so. The foregrounding may be done by formal devices of prosody, by syntagmatic deviance and by choice that is unexpected in the register.

Now we have seen that literature can and does avail itself of all registers in a *langue*; no register can be excluded—even though we may learn to recognize a distinctively literary register, or several. We do not know what to expect as we do in non-literary situations; we do not know where we are, and that is one reason why literature is exciting and important. Most communication in life is carried on with an unconscious prediction of probabilities and rejection of improbabilities. In buying a railway ticket, it is extremely likely that *single, please, change* will be heard, even more extremely unlikely that *dragon, tribal* or *syntax* will be. In a similar situation at a French station we could with some assurance exclude *tu*, though it might be very frequent in another situation. Nor is the determinant only semantic or social: it would be startling to hear *prognostication, disenchantment* or *glacial* in a weather forecast, though on some grounds they might seem quite appropriate.

No such inhibitions constrain the literary writer, and the response to his work must be open and receptive. Yet the balance is not all one way and although literature may seem open-ended in its possibilities, it does in fact act as something of a controlling influence. This is not, or not solely, by reason of prescriptivism among its practitioners and critics, but by the very fact of its existence as part of a community's culture, as a set of permanent and prestigious linguistic realizations. Sooner or later in every age, and despite the intentions of successive reformers, literature creates its own stylistic variations from the spoken norm.

Literary critics have perhaps been wiser than linguists in understanding what literature does for the words that it uses. Words which are lifted from the lexicon for a particular use may be returned to it with signs of their honour still upon them. A single use may dignify a word and give it life after many of its contemporaries have faded into archaism: this is true, for understanding if not for active use, of the Authorized Version *kine* and the Shakespearean *bourne*.

Misplaced revivals of the 'ye olde' type, however, leap from the holophrase like an obscenity. More often, the power of the word comes from repeated use. Think what Thackeray made of the obscure word *snob*, of how Wordsworth and the other Romantic poets conditioned our response to *nature*. Words are not things, but they can acquire associations which affect our way of understanding things.

Again the tension: for the word culled from the lexicon does not come untested by the speech-community. Like a human being, its distinctiveness is partly owed to the influence of birth and environment. Its user has a certain responsibility to honour its accepted meaning and its proper placing in the syntax. But these may not be beyond all doubt; usage can blur and blunt meaning as well as sharpening it, and the result may be the ambiguity against which manuals of good writing warn us and in which poets rejoice.

Since the publication of William Empson's *Seven Types of Ambiguity* in 1930, the word *ambiguity* has been used somewhat loosely in literary criticism to describe any feature in a text which could be interpreted in more than one way. There is no need to be over-fussy about nomenclature at this point, but it is as well to note that in linguistics *ambiguity* is usually taken with reference to the problem of sentences which seem identical in surface structure but have different deep meanings.

The ambiguities of daily speech are, generally, unintentional and call for clarification as soon as they are detected. They may be phonic—'I meant I'd have a pear, the fruit, not a pair, two'; or semantic—'Do you mean funny, peculiar, or funny, ha, ha?' or syntactic, as when we question whether *running water* means water which runs, or the process of causing water to run. Any of these may occur in literature, but in this style they are much more likely to be studied and intentional. The words of literary language may be in conflict, but it is conflict to which they are deliberately set on, in contrast to the random brawls of words in colloquial use.

The type of phonic ambiguity known as the *pun* is familiar to all. The phonic identity or close similarity of two or more words is exploited in a manner which brings their different meanings into juxtaposition. Its deterioration in the humour of the pantomime and the Victorian comic periodical should not make the modern reader despise its use in foregrounding with more serious intent. It can be explicit, when the words in question are realized as separate units:

> I'll gild the faces of the grooms withal,
> For it must seem their guilt.

> (*Macbeth*, II.i)

or implicit when we are left to deduce two meanings from one unit:

> This counsellor
> Is now most still, most secret, and most grave,
> Who was in life a foolish prating knave.

> (*Hamlet*, III.iv)

George Eliot has a fine use of the second type in *Daniel Deronda* (Chapter 23) when Gwendolen is distressed after a humiliating interview with Klesmer and her unsuspecting mother enters saying, 'I see by the wheel-marks that Klesmer has been here.' The surface meaning relates to 'the sound of his departing wheels getting more distant on the gravel' which Gwendolen has just heard, but the phonic identity with *weal* relates to the suffering which is not physical but has already been given a physical metaphor by the author— 'Every word that Klesmer had said seemed to have been branded into her memory'.

Literary ambiguity can draw on phonic, semantic and syntactic features. Shakespeare's punning on his own name with the complex Elizabethan associations of *will* with sexual as well as mental desire in Sonnet 143 is well known:

> So will I pray that thou mayst have thy Will.

Donne has an even more admirable piece of wordplay in 'A Hymn to God the Father' with its repeated refrain:

> When Thou has done, Thou hast not done;
> For I have more

and the conclusion:

> And having done that, Thou hast done;
> I fear no more.

Remembering the pronunciation of Donne as /d ∧ n/ we have here a use of language which heightens the uncertainty and spiritual anguish that is finally resolved by faith. It exploits the pun through the syntactic ambiguity of 'Thou hast', which could lead to the series:

> Thou hast done, finished, accomplished . . .

or to:

> Thou hast Donne, Herbert, Marvell . . .

The two series are equally possible in positive and negative verbs so that Donne offers us a complex dance of interpretations:

> When you have finished, you still have not got me . . .
> When you have got me, that is not the end . . .
> When you seem to have finished, you have not really ended . . .

and these are not all the possibilities. The point is that we do not seek the one 'correct' interpretation, for any meaning which the language can bear is correct within the poem.

A unit which most people would think of as 'one word' may carry a number of meanings, by association with certain contexts. Thus *pipe* can be any tubular object, a musical instrument or a piece of apparatus for smoking; a *hand* can be on a clock or watch as well as at the end of the arm. Multiple meaning or *polysemy* is of considerable linguistic importance, and the process of extension is a concern of historical linguistics. Most of the time, we are able to distinguish the intended meaning by the usual process of mental adjustment to context and register: we don't expect to find tobacco pipes in the school recorder band. The literary language, however, again refuses to give us comfortable divisions of meaning beyond which imagination need not stray. It often forces us to accept *polysemy* not as a feature from which we select but as one in which we meet the writer's intention without restriction. Thus Whitman in 'The Imprisoned Soul':

> At the last, tenderly,
> From the walls of the powerful, fortressed house,
> From the clasp of the knitted locks—from the
> keep of the well-closed doors,
> Let me be wafted.

We are not allowed to interpret *locks* solely as 'door locks' and exclude 'locks of hair' with its suggestion of binding human relationship. Although *fortressed* points to the architectural meaning of *keep*, the wider common sense of 'retention' is equally present.

The writer may indeed call in the aid of context to distinguish the meanings of polysemic words; but his intention is not necessarily to elucidate a single meaning but rather to emphasize the uncertainties of daily usage and to point from this to an ironical comment on the human predicament. What has already passed in the action allows us to follow the jealousy of Leontes through the meanings of *play* as 'reaction', 'sexual intercourse' and 'theatrical acting':

> Go, play, boy, play: thy mother plays and I
> Play too; but so disgraced a part, whose issue
> Will hiss me to my grave.
>
> (*The Winter's Tale*, I.ii)

A similar extension is made in Housman's poem, 'Lancer', with its repeated italicized line:

> *Oh who would not sleep with the brave?*

where the successive juxtapositions with other lines bring out the literal sense of the youth desiring comradeship of communal life, the sexual thoughts of the girls who watch the soldiers pass, and the sleep of death which is to be the recruit's fate.

Polysemy may allow a writer to work on two levels concurrently, apparently relating one set of events while really indicating something different. We move here towards metaphor, which must be a separate concern, but it is interesting to see how a chosen image can be maintained by word-choice appropriate to the register in which we should normally expect to find it, while the metaphorical relation to hidden meaning is deferred. For example, George Herbert sustains the image of God as the landlord in the poem 'Redemption' by use of legal terms which are in perfect register-agreement with the opening statement:

> Having been tenant long to a rich Lord
> Not thriving, I resolved to be bold,
> And make a suit unto him, to afford
>
> A new small-rented lease, and cancel th'old.
> In heaven at his manor I him sought:
> They told me there that he was lately gone

> About some land, which he had dearly bought
> Long since on earth, to take possession.

The overt legal narrative is acceptable in its own right but complacence is jarred by the intrusion of *heaven* and *on earth* and the reader is alerted for the conclusion:

> There I him espied
> Who straight, *Your suit is granted* said, and died

Here than is another example of register-mixing: we have already seen one in Henry Reed's 'Naming of Parts'. Selection is made of words current in more than one register of the speech community.

However, the writer may not confine himself to any normal register but rather create his own by choices that would seem odd or questionable in that context in everyday use. It is useful, though without attempting to draw any impassable line, to distinguish between two ways in which a writer's selection of a single word may seem admirable. We will assume that there is no syntagmatic deviation and that the choice is paradigmatic within a context that is free from apparent ambiguity. Of course, the associations and figurative applications of words may still operate even when there is no obvious polysemy.

In the first way, there is no deviation; the achievement is in tackling the problem of synonymous words. It may well be argued that there are no perfect synonyms, since choice must be conditioned by register, dialect and emotive association. However, the problem of word-selection is difficult and is not much aided by the brief definitions of a dictionary or the listings of a thesaurus. One of the most effective ways of finding out what a word means in current usage is by asking people whether they would readily use it in a given sentence. Consider the words in italics in each of the following quotations; space does not allow extended quotation, but it is advisable to look up the whole passage if possible. What other words could the writer have chosen which are seemingly synonymous? Would they have been equally effective, or more or less effective? This is the right sort of critical question to ask, although there is no single answer that is 'right' as a sum is right or wrong.

> A man so *various*, that he seemed to be
> Not one, but all mankind's, epitome.
>   (Dryden, *Absalom and Achitophel*)

Ten thousand saw I at a glance,
Tossing their heads in *sprightly* dance.

(Wordsworth, 'Daffodils')

Was she guilty or not? She said not; but who could tell what was truth which came from those lips; or if that *corrupt* heart was in this case pure?

(Thackeray, *Vanity Fair*, Ch. 18)

In that *enormous* silence, tiny and unafraid,
Comes up along a winding road the noise of the Crusade.

(Chesterton, 'Lepanto')

Last night at the Jackson's Agnes had displayed a *brisk* pity that made him wish to wring her neck.

(Forster, *The Longest Journey*, Ch. 26)

Against these we may set the choices that seem deviant because we should not normally regard them as available at the point of development which the text has reached. It is not that they come from a different register—that, as we have seen, is an easily detectable device—but rather that the paradigmatic list that we should expect to construct in order to choose a filler for this particular space would not contain it.

The blood-dimmed tide is loosed, and everywhere
The *ceremony* of innocence is drowned.

(Yeats, 'The Second Coming')

Here, we may feel, the metaphor of *tide* is well sustained in the participle *drowned*, and we are happy to accept a poetic personification of innocence, but *ceremony* pulls us up sharply. A rather rhetorical public speaker might use the same statement with *body of innocence*, or *figure*, or *person*, or *martyr*, or *victim* . . . We cast through the paradigm to find a word that can combine the abstraction of innocence with the physical nature of drowning in a tide. But Yeats was not prepared to close the list on these terms and he made a choice which was syntagmatically acceptable but which extended instead of further containing the metaphor of his vision. The reader may, if he wishes, say that the choice was a bad one; but the oddity of the choice foregrounds the word and demands that response to it is made.

Here are some more examples of paradigmatic deviance. The

reader will make his own response to them, based on the way in which he reacts to the defeat of regular linguistic expectation. It is necessary to consider the force of the chosen word in relation to other possibilities of the same class which might be considered more likely; also whether meaning is heightened or blurred by the deviation:

> But most through midnight streets I hear
> How the youthful harlot's curse
> Blasts the new-born infant's tear,
> And blights with plagues the marriage *hearse*.
>
> (Blake, 'London')

> Arthur followed him up the staircase . . . into a dim bed-chamber, the floor of which had gradually so sunk and settled, that the fireplace was in a *dell*.
>
> (Dickens, *Little Dorrit*, Bk. I, Ch. 2)

> I am the man who looked for peace and found
> My own eyes *barbed*.
>
> (Sidney Keyes, 'War Poet')

> Now as I was young and easy under the apple boughs
> About the *lilting* house and happy as the grass was green.
>
> (Dylan Thomas, 'Fern Hill')

The last quotation, of course, shows a second and more startling deviation by defeating expectation of the stereotyped simile 'happy as the day was long'. It brings us to consider the treatment which writers give another type of usage familiar in daily speech but often regarded as distinctively literary.

FURTHER READING

The important though difficult study of semantics can begin with G. N. Leech, *Towards a Semantic Description of English* (London, 1969, Longman), followed by S. Ullmann, *Semantics* (Oxford, 1962, Blackwell). R. A. Walrond, *Sense and Sense Development* (London, 1967, André Deutsch) is also useful. An older but influential work is C. K. Ogden and I. A. Richards, *The Meaning of Meaning* (10th ed., London, 1960, Routledge and Kegan Paul).

W. Empson, *Seven Types of Ambiguity* (London, 1930, Chatto and Windus) referred to on p. 64 is conveniently available in a cheaper edition (Harmondsworth, 1961, Penguin Books); see also Empson's later book, *The Structure of Complex Words* (London, 1951, Chatto and Windus).

The work of J. R. Firth is best approached through his *Papers in Linguistics 1934-51* (London, 1957, Oxford University Press); some of his ideas are developed by M. A. K. Halliday, A. McIntosh and P. Strevens, *The Linguistic Sciences and Language Teaching* (London, 1964, Longman).

Also useful are: C. S. Lewis, *Studies in Words* (Cambridge, 1960, Cambridge University Press); B. Groom, *The Diction of Poetry from Spenser to Bridges* (London, 1956, Oxford University Press); *Nowottny*, pp. 26-48, 146-73; *Leech*, pp, 42-4, 131-6, 105-21.

7

The Language of Rhetoric

The question of lexical deviation has emphasized something which has become increasingly apparent in the course of our study. Literary language does not function primarily for the purpose of conveying information verifiable by reference to experience which is not linguistic, or at all events not verbalized. Certainly this informative function is not excluded, and literature can increase our knowledge and understanding of the external world as discerned by sensory perceptions. Some literary fashions have made much of the need to be objectively 'true to life' and have earned such labels as 'realism' and 'naturalism', It does not demand much critical judgement, however, to distinguish this kind of creation from the factual reporting which makes no claim to be in the literary style.

A novel like Zola's *Germinal* or Upton Sinclair's *The Jungle* is much more—and also much less—than a report based on official interrogation and weighing of evidence. Much more, because it incorporates the author's desire to touch the emotions, to cause shock and to persuade into action; much less, because the 'facts' are selected and arranged in a way that does not totally reproduce a verifiable situation. The quality of imagination, which we have noted as one of the distinguishing marks of literature, comes into service. When it is not disciplined, the result is crude sensationalism; when it is inadequate, the result is a piece of non-literature in which the overt message is too much for the medium, as in many Victorian novels dedicated to a specific social reform.

The use of language to persuade or influence, even to promote action, is by no means inimical to literature. The fallacy of supposing that even non-literary language is primarily to inform has been assailed from Coleridge to Chomsky. The use of specific linguistic devices to make desired effects does not isolate literature from the common core of the *langue*. Close attention given in recent years to literary language has brought renewed respect for the attitude to 'style' which was dominant for a very long time in the past—the idea that literature produced a set of 'models' for the generation of desired linguistic effects. The study of *rhetoric* rested on a special kind of attitude to language as a faculty through which the recipient—reader or auditor—could be influenced in the manner desired by the writer or orator. Language could be manipulated into recognized 'figures', the categorizing and exemplifying of which was a proper concern of the critic from classical Greece to the beginning of the Romantic era. The relegation of these 'figures of speech' to textbooks, to be learned by rote and reproduced in examinations, gave them a bad name which they are now losing.

The attention of both critics and creative writers has been directed towards figurative language with a concern comparable to that shown in the sixteenth and seventeenth centuries. For the Renaissance writer, skill in rhetoric was a necessary part of the prevailing attitude to language in which excitement about newly discovered flexibility was in tension with anxiety about the status of the vernacular tongue. It was desirable that English should be proved capable of accommodating the figures traditional to Greek and Latin. Manuals like Peacham's *Garden of Eloquence* (1577) and Puttenham's *Art of English Poesy* (1589) did not seek to impose artificial constraints on creation but rather to codify contemporary practice and thereby guide both the poet and the daily user of language. The very fact of parody, as in Shakespeare's Sonnet which begins 'My mistress' eyes are nothing like the sun', proves the ready acceptance of rhetorical conventions. The strength of literature was seen to lie in its controlled use of features which did not destroy regular communication but were developed from familiar usage and arranged for the best effect.

All this is not far from the idea of foregrounding through deviation, with the related recognition of a *langue* as the totality of available resources from which different styles and dialects are drawn. So influential a critic as Northrop Frye has called for 'a wholesale revival of the lexicon of Renaissance rhetoric'. This lexicon may indeed help us to discuss the special kind of 'reality' which literature often presents: the creation of an experience pointing to no such perceivable objectivity as we might expect in a conversation or a news commentary, but unquestionably evoking response from the reader and becoming part of his individual situation.

F

This response requires no withdrawal from the instinctive response to specific performance by any member of the shared speech-community. It is not a switch of attention, but a further step in the distancing process which gives civilized language communicative value not possessed by the animal noise which automatically accompanies a given stimulus. Thus *lily* is not a white flower, but a sign which evokes our precedent knowledge of a white flower. This is the *denotative* use; a recipient with developed awareness of the language may let his thoughts dwell on the word *lily* and recall Pre-Raphaelite paintings and aesthetic notions of purity which are among the *connotative* associations. So he will be prepared to respond to Keats:

> I see a lily on thy brow,
> With anguish moist, and fever dew . . .
> ('La Belle Dame sans Merci')

with acceptance of the *figurative* use of the word, in which both denotative and connotative senses help to reach an understanding still farther away from the basic referent. Similarly, *branch* can aid communication about trees, can evoke ideas of dynamic growth in biological or political or religious registers, and can be accepted as purely figurative when used by Marlowe:

> Cut is the branch that might have grown full straight
> And burned is Apollo's laurel bough
> That sometime grew within this learned man.
> (*Doctor Faustus*)

In all this, as we have seen in other features of language, it is wiser to regard meaning as a spectrum rather than as a set of enclosed cells: figurative use does not emerge all of a sudden but shades off, both diachronically and synchronically, from connotation.

So once again the language of literature is seen to be not far from the conventions of daily speech and to be amenable to the same methods of investigation. Before looking at more literary examples, let us think further about the relationship of rhetoric to non-literary styles. The label 'figures of speech' was not such a misnomer as it appeared when these usages were tabulated in textbooks of prescriptive grammar. The apparent detachment was a result of the insistence that written language was the only type worthy of serious study, and of the raiding of past literature for examples to support names of figures which were treated as having reality in their own right.

Without departing from traditional nomenclature, or even traditional practice in adducing literary examples, we can find the figurative expressions alive in daily usage. There is no difficulty about agreeing with Bloomfield that 'poetic metaphor is largely an outgrowth of the transferred uses of ordinary language'. If we contend that the language of literature constitutes a style of the *langue*, any viable grammar must be able to accommodate the usages of literary writers. Conversely, the writers must be open to the judgement of the grammar.

We will look at some—not all—of the established figures in the dual relationship of literature and common usage. One distinction of types which has sometimes been overlooked is of considerable linguistic importance—the difference between *tropes* and *schemes* that was generally made by the great rhetoricians. Tropes depend essentially on paradigmatic relationships, schemes on syntagmatic. Most of the more familiar textbook 'figures of speech' are tropes. They take us on from the lexical deviations which were discussed at the end of the previous chapter and for which the name *metaphor* there became necessary. They are the result of unusual choices from the items which the grammar makes available in a given pattern.

Simile is the root-notion of tropes: the comparison derived from likeness perceived between two referents. There is clearly a very wide range of choice here, and the successful literary simile will point a likeness not usually discerned yet not so far-reached as to be purely subjective and therefore uncommunicative. At least one item generally refers to something perceptible by the senses, which foregrounds the other item by its actuality. The comparison may be directly between noun and noun:

> Thy soul was like a star, and dwelt apart:
> Thou hadst a voice whose sound was like the sea.
>
> (Wordsworth, 'London, 1802')

> She smiled as she saw how big his mouth was, and his chin so small, and his nose curved like a switchback, with a knob at the end.
>
> (Virginia Woolf, *The Voyage Out*)

or between a quality shared by the two items:

> His legions, angel forms, who lay entranced
> Thick as autumnal leaves that strow the brooks
> In Vallombrosa.
>
> (Milton, *Paradise Lost*, Book 1)

> Old as a coat on a chair; and his crushed hand
> as unexpressive as a bird's face.
>
> (Terence Tiller, 'Egyptian Beggar')

or between action which makes a verb act as the link:

> He trod the ling
> Like a buck in spring
> (Kipling, 'The Ballad of East and West')

> Words flower like crocuses in the hanging woods
> (Sidney Keyes, 'William Wordsworth')

All varieties are familiar in speech, repeated until worn into clichés: 'a face like thunder'; 'as cool as a cucumber'; 'March comes in like a lion and goes out like a lamb'.

Metaphor is a term sometimes used to include the more particular types of figure, such as those discussed below. While it may be convenient to consider them more specifically, they certainly have the nature of metaphor which makes analogy by compression of the simile so that the overt ground of likeness is not verbalized. The implicit comparison contained in a metaphor is the essence of figurative language and must be examined more closely later. For the moment a few examples will establish the relation of literary metaphor to common usage:

> I feed a flame within, which so torments me
> That it both pains my heart, and yet contents me.
>
> (Dryden, 'Hidden Flame')

> Thou still unravished bride of quietness,
> Thou foster-child of silence and slow Time
>
> (Keats, 'Ode on a Grecian Urn')

> But somewhere some word presses
> On the high door of a skull
>
> (Stephen Spender, 'Fall of a City')

A metaphor can be opened into simile and compressed again:

> (Mrs. Skewton) had a sharp eye, verily, at picquet. It glistened like a bird's, and did not fix itself upon the game, but pierced the room from end to end, and gleamed on harp, performer, listener, everything.
>
> (Dickens, *Dombey and Son*, Ch. 21)

Here the stereotyped 'sharp eye' metaphor develops into the animate simile of the bird, and the metaphoric possibilities of both ideas are exploited with 'pierced' and 'gleamed'.

Little comment is needed on the wide range of common metaphor, which falls into at least four degrees of being figurative in the awareness of users and recipients:

(i) The obvious and blatant metaphor which is always in danger of becoming ludicrous by associating with others in 'mixed metaphor' of the type, 'I smell a rat, I see it floating in the air, but I hope to nip it in the bud'.

(ii) The metaphor which is accepted as figurative because it puts an idea more vividly and forcefully than abstraction could do but does not seem seriously deviant in any register: 'in the light of experience', 'the hub of activity'.

(iii) The metaphor which is not regarded as figurative at all except when attention is drawn to it by gross 'mixing' or by the difficulty of finding a non-metaphorical word to fill the same space: 'the foot of the hill', 'a bottleneck in production', 'blanket legislation.'

(iv) The metaphor which is totally 'dead' because its literal meaning is lost or obsolescent and known only to the student of language: 'ponder', 'depend', 'preposterous'. This type is metaphorical only in a historical view.

Synecdoche is the metaphorical use of part of the referent to stand for the whole:

> Fair stood the wind for France
> When we our sails advance
> > (Michael Drayton, 'Agincourt')

> In came Mrs. Fezziwig, one vast substantial smile.
> > (Dickens, *A Christmas Carol*)

> Lay your sleeping head, my love,
> Human on my faithless arm.
> > (W. H. Auden, 'Lay your sleeping head')

The figure is familiar in everyday use such as 'hand' for 'workman'
—an example satirized by Dickens in *Hard Times*.

Metonymy is the use of some feature contiguous or closely
associated with the referent:

> Sceptre and Crown
> Must tumble down,
> And in the dust be equal made
> With the poor crooked scythe and spade.
>> (James Shirley, 'The glories of our blood')

> Cedant arma togae, concedant laurea laudi
>> (Cicero, *De Officiis*)

We accept daily such metonymy as 'Crown property'; 'coppers'
for small coins; and 'the pen is mightier than the sword', a quotation
from Bulwer Lytton that has become a cliché.

Meiosis is conscious understatement, with its special type **Litotes**
which uses a negative construction to foreground an intended
positive emphasis:

> He was a man, take him for all in all
>> (*Hamlet* I.ii)

> A thing of beauty is a joy for ever:
> Its loveliness increases; it will never
> Pass into nothingness.
>> (Keats, *Endymion*)

A very British turn of phrase: 'quite a few people', 'could be worse',
'not bad', 'by no means unlikely' . . .

Hyberbole is conscious overstatement which foregrounds the
theme by paradigmatic choices that would normally seem excessive
in the context:

> I will love thee still, my dear,
> Till a' the seas gang dry.
>> (Burns, 'My love is like a red, red rose')

> Cover her face; mine eyes dazzle: she died young
>> (Webster, *The Duchess of Malfi*, IV.ii)

A very un-British feature of ordinary speech? 'Terribly sorry'; 'it's
awfully good of you'; 'nobody could have been kinder' . . .

Tropes, then, are richly varied and unpredictable in the items which they include. Schemes make the foregrounding effect through development of normal syntactic patterns by repetition and juxtaposition; if they are deviant at all, it is by unusual frequency, not by unexpected choice. Rhetoricians have named many types of them; a very few must serve for illustration.

Anaphora, sometimes used of verbal repetition in general, is specifically the repetition of a word or phrase at the beginning of successive stages of the chosen pattern:

> After the torchlight red on sweaty faces
> After the frosty silence in the gardens
> After the agony in stony places
> (T. S. Eliot, *The Waste Land*)

> Now to the banquet we press;
> Now for the eggs and the ham;
> Now for the mustard and cress,
> Now for the strawberry jam!
> (W. S. Gilbert, *The Sorcerer*)

Dead, your Majesty. Dead, my lords and gentlemen. Dead, Right Reverends and Wrong Reverends of every order. Dead, men and women born with Heavenly compassion in your hearts.
(Dickens, *Bleak House*, Ch. 47)

Epistrophe uses repetition at the end of successive stages:

> If you did know to whom I gave the ring,
> If you did know for whom I gave the ring,
> And would conceive for what I gave the ring,
> And how unwillingly I left the ring,
> When naught would be accepted but the ring,
> You would abate the strength of your displeasure.
> (Shakespeare, *The Merchant of Venice*, V.i)

The device is very familiar in the refrains of songs and the repeated last line of stanzas in forms like the ballade.

Symploce repeats at the beginning and the end:

> We are the hollow men
> We are the stuffed men
> (T. S. Eliot, 'The Hollow Men')

and see also Wyatt's poem 'And wilt thou leave me thus?' which repeats this line at the beginning of each stanza and the line, 'Say nay! say nay!' at the end of each.

Anadiplosis links the end of one stage to the beginning of the next by repetition, as Donne's sonnets *La Corona* each take the last line of a sonnet to be the opening line of the next in the sequence. Ernest Dowson's 'Flos Lunae' opens and closes each stanza with the line 'I would not alter thy cold eyes'.

Epizeuzis repeats a word or phrase without any break at all:

> And when he falls, he falls like Lucifer,
> Never to hope again.
>
> (Shakespeare, *Henry VIII*, III.ii)

> Sun is torn in coloured petals on the water,
> The water shivering in the heat and the north wind
> (Rex Warner, 'Nile Fishermen')

We are certainly familiar with repetition in the syntax of daily speech; but we do not dignify it with technical names, in the way that we recognize the appearance of certain tropes. Repetition can be used consciously for emphasis—It's cold outside, bitterly cold'; or to establish a phatic sense of sharing—'It's a shame, isn't it?' 'Yes, it's really a shame.' More often, it is used unconsciously and is associated with users who have not a highly developed linguistic skill. Any overheard conversation in a public place is likely to yield the kind of repetition that Eliot reproduced in *The Waste Land*:

> When Lil's husband got demobbed, I said—
> I didn't mince my words, I said to her myself . . .

Nevertheless, patterned repetition is constantly found in literary language, and also in the religious register: for example, in litanies. Its appearance in the ritual and incantatory language of diverse cultures cannot be overlooked by the linguist.

It should now be clear that even the seemingly extreme usages of the literary style can be approached with the understanding that they grow from the common core of language. They do not call for modifications in the explanatory model of *langue*. They do, however, demand that we recognize the special dimension of literature in which these figures do not appear by automatic response or by rapid register-choice. They are planned and given performance as contributing to a situation in which creator and recipient share a linguistic act without sharing the outward event which is linguistically signified. The literary use of figurative language is evaluated in a whole text. In everyday speech, any figurative expressions can be paraphrased with no loss except possibly that of emphasis, or vivid effect, or suitability to register: the paraphrase of literary language loses what is essential to its kind of performance.

Equally, the response of the recipient is affected, but not limited, by his recognition that figures can occur in non-literary styles. The rules of interpretation which are applied almost automatically to the conversational use of 'I smell a rat' or 'as bold as brass' must be applied more carefully and thoroughly to gain the full appreciation of literary rhetoric. In speech we seldom consciously hold the literal and figurative meanings of an expression in balance at the same time, except when they are forced upon us by a deliberate pun or by accidental mixed metaphor. In the exploration of literature we learn to be on the alert for likenesses not seen before; and if the writer has done his work well, we have only the text itself to guide our awareness of the levels involved.

All that we have seen in respect of tropes has shown that some kind of *likeness* is the basis of every metaphor. It will be convenient now to consider *metaphor* as the basis of figurative language, without continually digressing to consider the more delicate sub-divisions of rhetorical theory. There must be some likeness, if metaphor is to communicate at all and not to lose all contact with reality. The point of contact between figurative and normative use may be very slight; and it is an indication of its success if it is one not realized before. Metaphor will focus attention on some aspect of the referent which makes analogy possible.

Metaphor often makes a bridge between levels of experience which are not normally considered to be expressible in the same terms. The bridging can be of many types: here by way of example are three of the most frequent.

(i) One type of sensory perception is expressed in terms of another:

> Annihilating all that's made
> To a green thought in a green shade
> > (Marvell, 'Thoughts in a Garden')

> If music be the food of love, play on
> > (Shakespeare, *Twelfth Night*, I.i)

> Her fist of a face died clenched on a round pain
> (Dylan Thomas, 'In Memory of Ann Jones')

and we may recall Chesterton's parody of modern verse:

> So sorry if you have a green pain
> Gnawing your brain away . . .
> When I have a pain,
> I never notice the colour.

(ii) A non-human referent is given human attributes:

> So I unto myself alone will sing;
> The woods shall to me answer, and my echo ring
> (Spenser, 'Epithalamion')

Flakes of soot . . . as big as full-grown snowflakes—gone into mourning, one might imagine, for the death of the sun.
(Dickens, *Bleak House*, Ch. 1)

(iii) An abstraction is treated as if it were animate;

> A terrible beauty is born
> (W. B. Yeats, 'Easter 1916')

> Bon chevalier masqué qui chevauche en silence,
> Le Malheur a percé mon vieux coeur de sa lance
> (Paul Verlaine, *Sagesse*, I)

In the analysis of metaphor we are in effect reconverting the thought back into the fuller statement of simile. A simile is tripartite: one thing is likened to another, and the ground of likeness is specified. The terms *tenor*, *vehicle* and *ground* have been applied in the elements of simile and the application will be shown in the following examples, where the superscribed T stands for 'tenor', V for 'vehicle' and G for 'ground':

> $\quad\quad\quad$ T $\quad$ G $\quad\quad$ V
> I have seen old ships sail like swans asleep
> (J. E. Flecker, 'The Old Ships')

> $\quad$ T $\quad\quad$ V $\quad\quad\quad$ G
> An eye like Mars to threaten and command
> (Shakespeare, *Hamlet*, III, iv)

T

His legions, angel forms, who lay entranced
G   V
Thick as autumnal leaves

(Milton, *Paradise Lost*, Bk. I)

Metaphor omits the ground, which has to be sought and supplied; it is in the kernel sentence but not found in the sentence as performed. Thus when we meet the metaphor that closes Auden's 'In Memory of W. B. Yeats':

In the prison of his days
Teach the free man how to praise

we supply the ground of constraint which links 'prison' with the inescapable progression of time verbalized as 'days'. Sometimes both tenor and ground must be supplied by the reader:

Their path lay upward, over a great bald skull, half grass, half stubble

(E. M. Forster, *The Longest Journey*, Ch. 12)

Here the vehicle 'skull' leads to the unexpressed 'hill', with the ground of shape and bareness. Frequently more than one step is needed to find the kernel:

Tiger, tiger, burning bright

(Blake, 'The Tiger')

'Bright tiger' is acceptable without recourse to metaphor; but we have to link the ground 'brightness' with the unexpressed vehicle 'fire', which leads to 'burning' as the actual item to be the vehicle:

(a) tiger (is as) bright (as a fire)
(a fire) burns bright
tiger burning bright

I hope that enough has been quoted to show that the freedom of choice in formation of metaphor is immense. Freedom must, however, be in tension with the linguistic restraints of syntax and lexicon discussed in previous chapters. Although, as we have seen, tropes are based on paradigmatic relationship and schemes on syntagmatic, yet every linguistic act is answerable to both systems. Randolph Quirk puts the point precisely:

> A metaphor involves simultaneously a *paradigmatic* relation between the literal element it replaces and the figurative one it introduces, and a *syntagmatic* relation between the literal and metaphorical elements in the linguistic environment.
>
> (*Minnis*, p. 308)

The purpose of stating a likeness creates a gap which has to be filled from the lexicon: the structure of the metaphor requires that the chosen item shall fit into the syntagmatic pattern. Thus, metaphor is not different in kind from other utterances for which, as we have seen, certain possibilities are open and others closed.

FURTHER READING

An excellent general introduction to the study of figurative language in literature is P. Dixon, *Rhetoric* (London, 1971, Methuen), which includes a useful bibliography.

I. A. Richards, *The Philosophy of Rhetoric* (London, 1936, Routledge and Kegan Paul), has been influential; it is the source of the terms 'tenor' and 'vehicle' used in this chapter.

C. Brooke-Rose, *A Grammar of Metaphor* (London, 1958, Secker and Warburg), is particularly good on analysis of the types of metaphorical analogy.

R. Wellek and A. Warren, *Theory of Literature* (London, 1949, Jonathan Cape), has an important study in Chapter 15, 'Image, Metaphor, Symbol, Myth'.

Some of the most valuable recent work on rhetoric with a stronger linguistic emphasis has been done by G. N. Leech: see *Leech*, pp. 73-86, and his 'Linguistics and the Figures of Rhetoric' (*Fowler*, pp. 135-56). *Nowottny*, pp. 49-98, should also be read.

For the Renaissance approach to the subject see L. A. Sonnino, *A Handbook to Sixteenth-century Rhetoric* (London, 1968, Routledge and Kegan Paul). Descriptions of the traditional figures as used in literary and formal writing will be found in H. W. Fowler, *A Dictionary of Modern English Usage* (Oxford, 1926, Oxford University Press).

8

Rhythm and Metre

The relationship between speech and writing has already been discussed as a concern of literary stylistics. Although the two modes of realization are distinct and not to be confused, the switch from one to another is not difficult in a literate society. The units of information do not precisely correspond in the two, but an alphabetical system of writing shows more or less an attempt to reproduce speech-sounds visually, although historical change and lack of phonetic understanding may result in something far short of perfection. It is possible to represent speech in writing by using alphabetical letters with the aid of diacritical marks, or extra symbols, or both: this is the basis of phonetic and phonemic transcription.

Yet phonemes, necessary as a concept in phonetic analysis, are not the only constituents of speech. Or to put it in less technical terms: our conversations do not consist only of sounds. There can be foreign learners of English—or any other tongue—who achieve faultless reproduction of the separate sounds but are almost unintelligible when they open their mouths. If each syllable in an utterance is given equal stress and an equal following pause, the recipient loses nearly all the features which enable meaningful response. An example would be the following sentence, here transcribed graphologically, in which the oblique strokes represent breath-pauses and the superscribed vertical marks represent breath-force or stress; no account is taken of the segmentation into 'words':

John/must/give/you/a/def/in/ite/an/swer/by/Fri/day

Leaving aside the difficulties of syllabic division in traditional spelling, it is clear that the pronunciation thus represented would not be heard in any native variety of English. To give any indication of actual utterance we have to show fewer pauses and greater variation in stress. By using a horizontal line for a light or secondary stress, and a cross for absence of stress, we can overcome at least some of the inadequacy of representation:

```
     |   ×   −  ×   × − × ×  |  ×   ×  |  ×
     Johnmustgiveyou/adefiniteanswer/byFriday
```

or, with different emphasis but no change of basic 'meaning':

```
  −    |  −   × × | × × × ×   ×  |  ×
     Johnmustgiveyou/adefiniteanswer/byFriday
```

A good many other arrangements of pause and stress are conceivable for this simple utterance within the bounds of normal conversation: it is clear that much more than a succession of sounds is involved. Elements of stress, pitch and duration make up the *intonation* which gives distinctive pattern to the dialects and idiolects of an ethnic language. It is chiefly through intonation that we are enabled to 'place' a person without necessarily understanding all that he says, or to parody the features of a foreign language which we speak imperfectly.

In graphological realization there is practically no indication of intonation; it is silently and subconsciously supplied by the reader, or inserted by the actor or reciter, helped to some extent by punctuation. A phonemic transcription cannot rely on ordinary punctuation which, although originally an aid to oratory, is incomplete and uncertain in the complexities of speech. A more delicate system of marking is used for these elements, which are the *supra-segmental* or *prosodic* division of phonetics. The word 'prosodic' at once reminds us that literary critics have for centuries been concerned with the regular patterns of verse and have tried to represent them visually by various systems of *scansion*.

For convenience we can use the word *rhythm* for the distinctive but variable pattern in the spoken utterances of a *langue*; the deliberate use of a regular and recurrent pattern in a literary composition will be called *metre*. General linguistic study is not concerned with metre as such, but metre can be examined linguistically in relation to the rhythm of spoken language. The latter is an extensive study and conclusions about it are by no means definitive; a few principles are important for the present.

We can recognize in speech the principle of 'equal timing' or *isochronism*, which breaks utterances into segments of approximately equal duration in sympathy with the pulses of breathing on which the sounds are produced. The segmentation is not the same in all languages; in French, for example, and more markedly in Japanese, it is syllabic. In English the unit is generally larger than the syllable, containing one stressed syllable and a variable number of unstressed. There are roughly equal time intervals from each stress to the next, though obviously not with metronomic precision. The different markings of the sentence examined above show how the system works, and also show that any major deviation from it breaks away from recognizable speech.

The main stresses tend to fall on form-words (nouns, verbs, adjectives, adverbs) rather than on the other parts of speech whose function is mainly grammatical or structural, and stress is thus closely related to the grammar and lexicon of the *langue*. This is not an infallible guide, however, particularly in English where stress can fall almost on any item that is to be foregrounded. For instance, if we give the instruction:

Put those books and papers on the table

the utterance is most likely to move fairly rapidly to find its main stress on *table*. It is, however, quite reasonable to say:

Put those books and papers on the table (not the others)

Put those books and papers on the table (not just the books)

Put those books and papers on the table (not underneath)

When we dwell too long on single examples out of context the result soon appears unreal or slightly comic, but unusual stressing is continually used in most conversations.

The duration which depends on stress must not be confused with the question of syllable-quantity; some syllables are longer than others because of their phonetic make-up, apart from whatever length is imposed on them in connected utterance by force and pause of breathing. Thus *sit* /sit/ is shorter than *seat* /si:t/ which in turn is shorter than *seed* /si-d/; two consonants give greater length to the preceding vowel than does a single consonant—*Stan* is shorter than *stand*. This factor enters into the total prosodic effect of an utterance.

Another feature of speech is the apparently negative but actually very important one of silence. It appears in the brief pauses between segments and the longer ones between sentences, the latter units not always corresponding to the syntactic structure that would qualify as a sentence in traditional grammar. A tape-recording of conversation will reveal pauses of considerable duration of which the original participants were not aware at the time. Within an utterance, the placing of a brief pause can distinguish the different meanings of identical sequences of phonemes which may or may not be fully distinguishable by context:

> some addresses   :   summer dresses
> take Greater London   :   take Grey to London

Literary critics and theorists were aware of such prosodic features long before any scientific study of speech was made. There have been a number of theories about exactly how English poetry is constructed and consequently how it can best be scanned. Many of the theories, like those developed in formal grammar, have leaned too heavily on the classical languages and obscured the close relationship between literary and spoken English. There was for a long time concentration on the feature just noted of syllable quantity, which was the basis of Latin verse prosody. The Romantics, with their principle—at least in the first generation—of bringing poetry back to daily speech-rhythm, looked to what Coleridge in the preface to 'Christabel' called 'a new principle: namely that of counting in each line the accents, not the syllables'. The principle was perhaps new in theory rather than in practice, but it became important in nineteenth-century thinking about prosody. There was a revival of interest in the accentual metre of Old English poetry, which had depended on a fixed number of stresses in each line, with considerable freedom in the number of unstressed syllables.

We have already seen that this is in fact the basis of English speech-rhythm. Students of English literature will be familiar with the elaboration of the basic theory in Old English, its debased form in the alliterative metre of the later medieval period as used by Langland, and its transformation into the 'sprung rhythm' of Gerard Manley Hopkins. What Hopkins wrote about his theory of prosody, as well as his actual poetry, is interesting source-material for literary stylistic study. Some examples have been quoted in earlier chapters as illustrative of other features and may be re-examined, bearing in mind that he worked on the basis of stresses which could follow one another without intermission or be separated by an indeterminate number of unstressed syllables. Unlike the Old English poets, he sometimes used rhyme and did not always incorporate alliteration of the stressed syllables. If his poetry is read aloud with the confidence of consecutive but planned speech, it presents fewer difficulties than its appearance on the printed page may suggest. The same is true of many other late Victorian and more recent poets who did not expatiate so fully on their prosodic theories.

There is of course no lack of theories at present; perhaps there have never been so many serious attempts to find out what lies beneath the writing of verse. There is no place here for the exploration of different approaches. If we stick to the simplest idea of stress-metre we shall have to exclude many important ideas for the sake of simplicity. Once we have looked carefully at the relationship of metre to language, however, the way is open for further work. There is a great deal of argument about metrics, but general agreement that the subject can be explored linguistically and that it does relate to familiar speech.

That pure stress metre is 'natural' to English is indicated by its adoption in nursery rhymes and children's communal play-rhymes:

׀   ׀   ׀   ׀

There was an old woman that lived in a shoe

׀   ׀   ׀   ׀   ׀

Wee Willy Winkie runs through the town

׀   ׀   ׀   ׀

April Fool's gone and past,

׀   ׀   ׀   ׀

You're the biggest fool at last

These clearly follow spoken stresses and not any regular pattern of syllabic stress. Yet their users are aware that they are somehow 'different' from ordinary talking and that the satisfaction which they give demands greater attention to stress placement. In fact the child knows, of course without precise formulation, that poetic composition rests on two sorts of pattern. There is the rhythm which gives the intonation by which speech is accepted as 'normal' in a national or local community, and there is the metre which follows more precise patterns and can be given the codification of 'rules'.

G

Rhythm can, and most frequently does, exist without metre: but metre draws its being from the existence of rhythm.

In the divisions of literature metre is considered an adjunct of *verse*—a term which will suffice to make the technical distinction from *prose* without creating any difficulties about the boundaries of *poetry*. Prose shares the quality of rhythm, in the sense in which we have been associating it with spoken intonation. Anything which is consistently written in metre, then, ceases by definition to be prose; but the appearance of occasional metre in prose can be the result either of chance or of design: more often, perhaps, of a spilling over from exceptionally sensitive awareness of normal rhythm. We are most likely to become aware of metre in prose when reading aloud, but the pattern may be strong enough to present itself even in silent reading and to invite scansion:

```
 ×    –   |  ×    ×   –  |     ×     –   | ×   ×   –  |  ×
O poor mortals,/ how ye make/ this Earth bitter/ for each other
```
(Carlyle, *The French Revolution*, V, 5)
```
 ×   –  | ×    ×    –    ×  | ×    ×    ×  |   –   |    × –
No more firing/ was heard at Brussels/ the pursuit/rolled miles away
```
(Thackeray, *Vanity Fair*, Ch. 33)

There is need for more work yet on the questions of metre in prose; so far no effective notation has been developed, so that analysis is compelled to depend on the scansion used for verse, which soon proves too rigid for more than a brief extract. George Saintsbury in his time pursued the problem with vigour but his findings were over-elaborate and sometimes clearly idiosyncratic. It is pretty certain that closer linguistic study will cause some revision of the demarcation between verse and prose, as we learn more about the patterns of speech rhythm. It is salutary to remember that understanding of Hebrew poetry, with its characteristic patterning through types of parallelism, was lost in translation until Louth rediscovered it some two hundred years ago.

Even in the days of most rigid classical prescriptivism, however, the poets themselves were seldom so far removed in their practice from ordinary speech rhythm as the Romantics and their disciples may have believed. Our leading poets have constantly, in their own terms, echoed the judgement of Robert Graves: 'One of the most difficult problems is how to use natural speech rhythms as variations on a metrical norm'. (*The Crowning Privilege*). We can look back long before Wordsworth and Coleridge, to the best later medieval poetry—to Chaucer who 'knew that a poet could avoid dullness by using the rhythms of common speech'.[1]

The comparatively barren period in literature which followed Chaucer, accompanied by changes in the English language, led to the metrical uncertainty of Wyatt and Surrey—though Wyatt may have been more consciously concerned to bring the spoken rhythm into his work—and Skelton's monotonous clutching at frequent stresses. Early dramatic blank verse over-compensated by a series of regular lines, 'end-stopped' so that sense and metre generally pause together:

> And thus experience bids the wise to deal.
> I lay the plot, he prosecutes the point,
> I set the trap, he breaks the worthless twigs
> And sees not that wherewith the bird is limed.
>> (Thomas Kyd, *The Spanish Tragedy*, III.iv)

Here we are only too aware of five stresses in each line, each alternating with an unstressed syllable: it is a different kind of verse from that of the later Shakespeare and his contemporaries:

> Why, 'tis impossible thou canst be so wicked,
> Or shelter such a cunning cruelty,
> To make his death the murderer of my honour.
> Thy language is so bold and vicious,
> I cannot see which way I can forgive it
> With any modesty.
>> (Thomas Middleton, *The Changeling*, III.iv)

Nor was the change felt only in dramatic verse; the Elizabethan lyric was often drawn towards the steady beat of music rather than the looser rhythm of speech; for example:

> Upon my lap my sovereign sits
> And sucks upon my breast;
> Meantime his love maintains my life
> And gives my sense her rest.
> Sing lullaby, my little boy,
> Sing lullaby, mine only joy.
>> (Richard Rowlands, 'Lullaby')

[1] A. C. Partridge, *The Language of Renaissance Poetry* (London, 1971, André Deutsch), p. 29.

The stresses follow the controlled movements of the hand on the lute; it needed Donne to bring back to the lyric the pulses of breath with minor syllables clustered around each emphasis:

> I wonder, by my troth, what thou and I
> Did till we loved? were we not weaned till then?
> But sucked on country pleasures, childishly?
> Or snorted we in the seven sleepers' den?

Other periods of literature can yield similar examples of poetry drawing closer to speech rhythm or diverging from it. If the divergence gives the kind of poetry that can be called 'artificial', this need not correspond with a critical response of good versus bad. Whether poetry should always be close to current speech is a question not to be answered by a simple axiom; what is certain, however, is that metre assumes an important function when it makes us most aware of underlying speech rhythm. It restores to poetry some of the immediacy that is lost by formal graphological presentation. It works, with the syntactic and lexical features that we have discussed, to meet expectation with surprise.

For metre can disturb the normal run of emphasis, just as the breath-force in speech can be directed onto structural words which are normally unstressed. The stresses of metre can give unexpected prominence to a syllable, and corresponding lightness to another. It can thus foreground items which have no apparent lexical or grammatical support. In the following examples, the italicized syllables have metrical prominence which gives, respectively, strong negation; exclamatory appeal; and the contrast between a verb used successively in positive and negative form which is commonly found in speech:

> No, *no*, go *not* to Lethe, *nei*ther twist
>
> Wolfsbane, tight-rooted, for its poisonous wine
> (Keats, 'Ode to Melancholy')
>
> My mother bore me in the southern wild,
>
> And I am black, but *O*, my soul is white
> (Blake, 'The Little Black Boy')

$$\times \quad | \times \quad | \times \quad - \quad | \quad - \quad \times \quad | \times \times$$
To *be* or *not* to be, that is the question

(*Hamlet*, III.i)

(In Shakespeare's time, *question* was trisyllabic.)

Further, this foregrounding can link items or anticipate con-nections which might otherwise be missed. There is no need to work out the whole scansion to understand what is done by metrical stress to aid progressive tension here:

> The *first* word that Sir Patrick read
> So loud, loud, laughed he;
> The *next* word that Sir Patrick read
> The tear blinded his e'e.

(Anon., 'Sir Patrick Spens')

or indeed in this more sophisticated example from Clough's *Amours de Voyage*:

> But a man was *killed*, I am told, in a place where I *saw*
> *Some*thing; a man was *killed*, I am told, and I *saw some*thing

The bewilderment and would-be detachment of the narrator forced to the centre of violence is foregrounded by the repeated contrast of the verbs *killed* and *saw*, associated with stress on the normally uncertain prefatory syllable *some-*.

There is of course a danger of elevating the unusual or deviant to higher critical evaluation than the regular, in metrics as in all stylistic examination. This is particularly so when we consider the relationship between the verse-unit and the syntactic unit. Verse is graphologically set out as *lines* (*verses* is the technically more proper term, but may be confusing) which can be shown to have phonic end-markers such as rhyme or a clear breath-pause. The line-ending may coincide with a natural break in the syntagmatic progression or may cut across it; the former type is seen in the examples above from Kyd and Rowlands, the latter in the one from Middleton. But end-stopping is not confined to tentative or inadequate verse; it is frequent in Shakespeare's sonnets—'Shall I compare thee to a summer's day?' is a good example. Nor does a poet deal only in end-stopping or in running-on (*enjambement*): he may employ both in the same poem. The manipulation of the two, with the resultant tension between the expected and the surprising, is part of the appeal. In the following extracts, the syntactic pauses are shown by vertical lines in the text and are seen to vary between line-endings and points within the lines:

> I cannot see what flowers are at my feet, |
> Nor what soft incense hangs upon the boughs, |
> But, | in embalmed darkness, | guess each sweet
> Wherewith the seasonable month endows
> The grass, the thicket and the fruit-tree wild |
> > (Keats, 'Ode to a Nightingale')

> At the round earth's imagined corners, | blow
> Your trumpets, Angels, | and arise, arise
> From death, you numberless infinities
> Of souls, | and to your scattered bodies go |
> > (Donne, *Holy Sonnets*, 7)

> That's my last Duchess painted on the wall,
> Looking as if she were alive; | I call
> That piece a wonder now: | Fra Pandolf's hands
> Worked busily a day, | and there she stands. |
> > (Browning, 'My Last Duchess')

This conflict between pauses where speech would not make them and pauses forced into metrical pattern by awareness of speech rhythm, with intermittent release when both types of pause coincide, is part of the poetic secret. The technique of the conflict will vary between one language and another, according to the nature of normal speech segmentation. It is arguable that certain verse-units are 'right' for certain national tongues; they seem close to the patterns of daily speech and are thus able to accommodate a good deal of end-stopping without monotony. This may be true for English of the iambic pentameter, which certainly occurs quite frequently in non-literary conflicts and can be inserted into verse without change. The consequent shock is not a metrical one:

> At last he rose and twitched his mantle blue:
> The stated price is subject to review.

> Yes, I am proud; I must be proud to see
> Results will be announced at half past three.

But that which is so gross a change of style in Milton or Pope may be less apparent elsewhere:

> Grave Jonas Kindred, Sybil Kindred's sire,
> Was six feet high, and looked six inches higher.

Is the second line added as a parody? George Crabbe intended it to follow the first as poetry, and the fact that it gives pause by its too-close resemblance to daily speech may tell us someting more about the distinctive style of literary language. Similar effects may occur in other languages; even the stately alexandrine of Racine is in danger:

> Quelques crimes toujours précèdent les grands crimes.
> Quiconque a pu franchir les bornes légitimes,
> Peut violer enfin les droits les plus sacrés—
> Le train ne peut partir que les portes fermées

Poetic tension demands a line which is not too far from speech rhythm but which can avoid monotony or bathos. The poets have in fact subjected the iambic pentameter and other lines to a great deal of variation: it will be found that scansion in the so-called 'iambic foot' ($\times$|) is seldom possible for long stretches and that what we in fact find is a line of five stresses isochronously separated by an irregular number of half-stressed or unstressed syllables—a pattern closer to speech and to the old accentual metre. Similar adaptation to speech rhythm is generally made by those who have adopted unusual or neo-classical lines—such as the loose hexameters of Clough quoted above, or Tennyson in 'Locksley Hall' or Byron in 'The Destruction of Sennacherib'.

The role of prosody is in the 'performance' of a poem—not necessarily or usually in reciting aloud, when the metrical pattern becomes most apparent, but in every encounter with it as a piece of language drawn from the same common stock that provides for our own performances in everyday speech. A reader who is sensitive to the intonations of speech may gain most from a poem: conversely, familiarity with a nation's poetry is one way of becoming familiar with its spoken nuances.

If metre can be said to impose rules on the norm of rhythm, it can also break its own rules and use deviation for effect to replace or

complement the literary deviations in lexis or syntax. The alexandrine, little used as a regular line in English, appears at the end
of every Spenserian stanza, and occasionally makes a triplet out of
the Augustan heroic couplet, marking a stronger pause in the flow
that could become monotonous, and foregrounding the content of
the deviant line. A similar pause, dramatically intended, may be
made by an incomplete line in blank verse:

> Tears in his eyes, distraction in's aspect,
> A broken voice, and his whole function suiting
> With forms to his conceit. And all for nothing.
> For Hecuba?
> What's Hecuba to him or he to Hecuba,
> That he should weep for her? What would he do,
> Had he the motive and the cue for passion
> That I have? He would drown the stage with tears . . .
>
> (*Hamlet*, II.ii)

In the next example, like a change of key in music or of register in
speech, a monosyllabic iambic pentameter switches response from
the loose, conversational metre of chattering monologue to the
overtly 'poetic' language and imagery of a different level of reverie:

> Shall I part my hair behind? Do I dare to eat a peach?
> I shall wear white flannel trousers and walk upon the beach
> I have heard the mermaids singing, each to each.
>
> I do not think that they will sing to me.
>
> I have seen them riding seawards on the waves
> Combing the white hair of the waves blown back
> When the wind blows the water white and black.

So, with T. S. Eliot's 'Love Song of J. Alfred Prufrock', we come
to the period in which 'free verse' has been the dominant poetic
form. Free verse will seem to be at best totally deviant, at worst to
be indistinguishable from prose, if we try to scan it by the rigid
patterns which have been shown as often inapplicable even to
traditional poetry. It is in fact a further development of the formal-
izing of speech rhythm, less predictable and regular, frequently
syncopated in metre as in syntax, but not by any means anarchic.
It is full of surprises, but even the surprises can often be seen as a
development from traditional metres. It may not be capable of

scansion by regular stress, or syllabic stress, or syllabic quantity, but it has not eschewed these and other prosodic features.

One characteristic of free verse is clearly shown graphologically in the occurrence of short lines and irregular spacing. We may take these not as untidiness but as a careful use of the silent stresses which are detectable in traditional metres. The iambic penameter often cannot be made to produce five full stresses without distortion; one stress may fall silently on a marked pause which keeps the isochronous pace of the line; it is marked by asterisks in the following examples:

    × | ×   ×   − | | | ×   × |
    The oldest hath borne most * we that are young

    × | × | ×   − | × | × |
    Shall never see so much * or live so long
                              (*King Lear*, V.iii)

    × | × | | ×   × − | × × |
    He scarce had ceased * when the superior fiend
             (Milton, *Paradise Lost*, Book 1)

Such pauses in free verse should be observed in 'performance', when they are found to create their own kind of tension and often to form part of blank verse lines:

    − | × | × ×   × − | |
    I climbed through woods in the hour-before-dawn dark.

    | × | × | − × | × |
    Evil air, a frost-making stillness *

    −   × | − × | | | |
    Not a leaf, not a bird— * * *

    × | − × | | × | | ×− × |
    A world cast in frost. * I came out above the wood.
             (Ted Hughes, 'The Horses')

Free verse, by its nature, offers more opportunities of differing metrical interpretations than do traditional forms. Another reader may 'hear' the stresses and pauses differently without one being plainly right and the other wrong. Perhaps we shall in time develop a new system of scansion and notation with some evaluative facility for modern forms: even now there are several suggested ways. Every system, however, seems to relate verse form and speech rhythm and to find in free verse the patterning which must distinguish

it from prose. Of course not all free verse is disciplined to this extent:
nor was all regularly metrical verse poetically inspired. Here are
two examples in which freedom and discipline go together. The first
is little if any freer than much Jacobean blank verse; the second is
looser, but with the freedom of carefully planned intonation.

```
    |     ×  –   |    ×   | × × |  × – |
What is your want, perpetual invalid *
×    |  ×  |  ×  |  ×  |  ×  –  ×  |
Whose fist is always beating on my breast's
|    |    ×   | × ×    –   | × × ×      |
Bone wall, incurable dictator of my house
  ×   |   ×   × ×  |    |    | ×    –    |
And breaker of its peace? * What is your will,
  ×   | ×  | ×    |      |     –  ×  |
Obscure uneasy sprite: where must I run,
    |   –  × |   | | ×  |
What must I seize, * * to win
×   |   |  × ×     –    × | ×    |    |
A brief respite from your repining cries? *
                    (David Gascoyne, 'The Writer's Hand')


  ×     |     | × ×   × |  × ×  | ×   ×  |
The King's poet was his captain of horse in the wars.
×    |  – ×  × |     | ×  |
He rode over the ridge: * his force
 –  | ×   × |  × ×    |    |   ×  | ×
sat hidden behind, as the king's mind had bidden.
  ×    |   ×  –   |   ×   | × ×  × |  ×
The plain below held the Dragon in the centre,
  |  × –  × × |  × ×  |      | –
Lancelot on the left, on the right Gawaine,
 |  × × |  ×   | ×   ×  |   × |
Bors in the rear commanding the small reserve.
                    (Charles Williams, 'Mount Badon')
```

FURTHER READING

Prosody has attracted a great deal of critical attention in recent
years. A good introduction is G. S. Fraser, *Metre, Ryhme and Free*

Verse (London, 1970, Methuen). The work of George Saintsbury referred to on p. 90 is still worth reading, most conveniently in his *Historical Manual of English Prosody* (London, 1910, Macmillan) and *History of English Prose Rhythm* (London, 1912, Macmillan). A comprehensive modern survey is K. Shapiro and R. Beum, *A Prosody Handbook* (New York, 1960, Harper and Row).

A specifically linguistic approach is made in two important but difficult books: E. Epstein and T. Hawkes, *Linguistics and English Prosody* (Buffalo, 1959, Buffalo University Press) and S. Chatman, *A Theory of Meter* (The Hague, 1964, Mouton).

Useful articles are R. Fowler, 'Prose Rhythm and Metre' (*Fowler*, pp. 82-99); P. J. Wexler, 'Distich and Sentence in Corneille and Racine' (*Fowler*, pp. 100-17); H. J. Diller, 'Linguistic Observations on the Heroic Couplet in English Poetry' in G. E. Perren and J. L. Trim, eds., *Applications of Linguistics* (London, 1971, Cambridge University Press), pp. 181-8; *Leech*. pp. 103-28.

The prosodic element in English speech is studied fully in D. Crystal, *Prosodic Systems and Intonation* in English (London, 1969, Cambridge University Press); the main interest for readers of this book is the chapter 'Past Work on Prosodic Features', pp. 20-96.

Two very useful papers by a phonetician appear in D. Abercrombie, *Studies in Phonetics and Linguistics* (London, 1965, Oxford University Press): 'A Phonetician's View of Verse Structure', pp. 16-25 and 'Syllable Quality and Enclitics in English', pp. 26-34.

The quotation on p. 90 is from Lecture 4 of R. Graves, *The Crowning Privilege* (London, 1955, Cassell); the whole section is well worth reading.

For more information on Hopkins see M. M. Holloway, *The Prosodic Theory of Gerard Manley Hopkins* (Washington, D.C., 1947, Catholic University of America Press).

9
Beyond the Sentence

Sentences have been described by H. Weinreich as 'the Hercules columns of linguistics' (*Chatman: Style*, p. 221), in recognition of the fact that recent linguistic theory has tended to deal with no unit larger than the sentence. A grammar is regarded as satisfactory if it can generate all, and only, the acceptable sentences of a language. There has been much attention to the phonemes and morphemes from which sentences are formed, comparatively little to sequence of sentences.

It is plain to everyone, linguists and non-linguists alike, that very little human communication through language is confined to isolated sentences. The concern of literary criticism in particular is with the total text which constitutes a 'work' of the author, whether it be as short as a Japanese *haiku* or as long as *War and Peace*. The exercise of reducing a work, or a section of it, to its basic components is a valuable means of finding informed response to the whole. The 'pieces' of a literary work are as interesting as the separate parts of a complex machine and as essential for understanding. The student whose concern is mainly literary may think that they are about as useless too, once they are parted from the total structure.

In fact stylistics, whatever style is being investigated, cannot proceed very far without recognition of units above the sentence. Even the brief examples used in previous chapters have sailed a little way beyond the Hercules pillars without, it is hoped, falling over the edge of the discoverable world. A unit of linguistic performance which stands complete in itself is commonly called a *discourse*. The name gives no information about size, style or quality. At the lower end of the scale it can be a single imperative—'Stop!'—and the upper end is completely open as far as analysis is concerned, depending on factors of planning and endurance which are not linguistic phenomena. A discourse is the effective or, in Halliday's description, 'operational' unit of language, as the sentence is the syntactic unit. To be of more than immediate and limited value in communication, a sentence must stand in relation with other sentences. Yet the sentence is not merely a theoretical unit: we reach the fullness of a discourse, however long, through a linear progression of sentences encountered in the order which the performer gives them.

The main reason why comparatively little work has been done on discourse is the difficulty of creating linguistic 'models' from which a kind of grammar of discourse could emerge. We simply do not know enough about how sentences build up into larger units. So at this point, of vital importance for stylistic study, we are left to use a good deal of common intellegence about communication, some of the traditional approaches to whole texts, and the sense of exciting research in progress.

The reader may care to look at some of the work done by Z. S. Harris, to whom we owe the term 'discourse analysis', and the following definition:

> Discourse analysis is a method of seeking in any connected discrete linear material, whether language or language-like, which contains more than one elementary sentence, some global structure characterising the whole discourse (the linear material), or large sections of it.

Particulars of the short but important work from which this quotation comes are given at the end of the chapter. The reader should be warned that Harris works mainly on technical rather than literary texts and that much of his analysis has a forbiddingly diagrammatic appearance. It is, however, a pointer to the kind of work which linguists are likely to attempt more and more in the future.

In dealing with the approach to whole works, the lack of space for extended quotation is obviously a handicap. The next step is to make a few general observations, with only minimal reference, in the hope that the reader will go to the texts to verify—or perhaps dispute—the assertions that are made.

First—and this is commonsense but needs to be kept in mind— a discourse may reveal meaning and significance which is not apparent in the isolated sentence. A sequence of words which has the appearance of an unacceptable sentence may prove acceptable in a completed structure. The foreign learner who says 'I'll make my possible' for 'I'll do my best' is told that he is being completely unidiomatic. But an interviewer of candidates for admission to a course might well say at the end of the proceedings, 'I'll make my possible acceptances into an alphabetical list.' Literature gives sentences which yield only partial comprehension on first encounter but which show richer significance when the work is fully known.

'I thought the King had more affected the Duke of Albany than Cornwall.' Kent's words that open *King Lear* convey very little to the reader or auditor coming to the play for the first time: they compose a gramatically well-formed sentence with obscure semantic reference. It requires five acts to reveal the full sense of those proper nouns.

Next, any discussion of recurrent linguistic features must take account of the whole discourse if it is to be at all useful. Leo Spitzer counselled the student to read over a text many times until he recognized one or more recurrent stylistic idiosyncrasies, which he would then try to explain from the writer's psychology. The final assault on the work was to return with this knowledge and look for its appearance in yet other features. This is a method which perhaps leaves too much to the reader's own psychological presuppositions; but it demands close and repeated attention to the whole discourse, without which no critical conclusions are worth much.

The pursuit of a single word, phrase or image through the discourse can be valuable in two ways. First it can, as Spitzer suggested, lead to better understanding of the author's whole achievement. Additional information from outside the text, not necessarily only psychological, can illuminate the discourse and the discourse can in turn confirm what is known externally. Yeats uses the rare word 'gyre' in more than one poem and his usage links with non-poetic statements of his personal mythology in which cyclic notions play a considerable part. Or the occurrence of the word 'sweet' more than thirty times in Shakespeare's *Sonnets* leads to consideration not only of his own affective response to life but also to the description of him as 'Sweet Mr. Shakespeare' in the contemporary *Return from Parnassus* and to the praise of Francis Meres—'the sweet witty soul of Ovid lives in mellifluous and honey-tongued Shakespeare . . . his sugared sonnets'.

The significance of the recurrent feature may be purely internal to the discourse, as when a character is given a keyword or catchphrase which identifies him and perhaps adds to his convincing existence. Dickens frequently works the trick—and indeed over-works it—as with Captain Cuttle's 'When found, make a note on' and Miss Mowcher's 'volatile'. In Iris Murdoch's novel *The Bell*, the sixth-form schoolboy Toby applies the adjective 'rebarbative' to a variety of people, things and situations. His first use of it seems unlikely and out of character; only through the whole novel do we come to understand that he has recently added it to his vocabulary and that its repetition and pejorative sense precisely express his immature but observant and critical character.

In this kind of analysis statistical methods can be useful and have been employed particularly in attempts to check questions of disputed authorship. It will be apparent that the *pleremes* ('full words' like nouns, verbs, adjectives and adverbs) will be of main importance and we must not expect too much from recurrence of the words in other classes—the *kenemes*—whose function is mainly syntactic. Yet these last cannot be neglected and have been found significant in some analyses. For instance, the definite article occurring with great frequency may indicate a desire to particularize and be specific rather than general: George Rostrevor Hamilton found it so in his study of modern poetry, *The Telltale Article*.

As well as the recurrence of words and phrases, discourse analysis must consider syntactic recurrence and sentence-pattern. One example of the former is George Herbert's frequent use of the first-person past definite to open a poem; a glance at the index of first lines in *The Temple* will confirm this and, I hope, impel the reader to further investigation. Herbert had come to this devotional serenity from years of debate about whether to take holy orders; he continually sees himself in past action of rebellion, defiance or lack of faith. Another example, which subsumes a good deal of the Romantic response to life, is the frequency of direct apostrophe to animal or inanimate themes in the two generations of the English Romantic poets. For recurrent patterns of sentence structure, the reader is referred to studies cited at the end of the chapter.

Since we are again dealing with the sentence, it is important to remember that the linguistic content of a sentence may not con-form to the graphological realization of a sequence of words starting with a capital letter and ending with a full stop. Many of these written 'sentences' are really two or more sentences in their deep structure. Harris gives the example from his analysis of Thurber's story 'The Very Proper Gander' in which the sentence:

He was strutting in his front yard, singing to his children and
his wife

is a transform of:

He was strutting in his front yard, he was singing to his children
and his wife

and the second part is a further transform of:

He was singing to his children and he was singing to his wife.

This kind of understanding helps us to determine what structures
and patterns really make up a discourse under consideration. Readers
who are familiar with Chomsky's methods of transformation may
wish to use them; but simpler methods of arriving at the kernels of
meaning can be stylistically perfectly valid.

Now it is clear that, whether or not a given sentence can be
divided, a sequence of sentences must be connected to create a
discourse. Everyone is accustomed to recognize and name units
beyond the sentence: the paragraph in prose, the stanza in verse.
The existence of verse-paragraphs as stylistic units is also recognized;
such divisions are often marked graphologically in modern poetry
and can be discerned in the long poems without stanza-divisions of
Milton, Dryden, Pope, Wordsworth, Browning and a great many
others. Beyond these we have the divisions proper to the different
literary 'kinds': chapters, scenes and acts, cantos and books. Every
unit depends on two factors: connection and silence.

To take connection first, we have the opinion of Coleridge that 'a
close reasoner and a good writer in general may be known by his
connectives'. Without going so far, it is apparent that connectives
are among the essential features of discourse: a random order of
sentences which were themselves well-formed would be meaningless.
Each sentence in a discourse is a step forward in the linear material
which Harris describes: it is also a glance back at what has just been
formulated. Understanding depends on overt or concealed reference
to the precedent. There is no established list of connectives; how
many are observed depends largely on the precision with which
minor differences are categorized. Here are some of the most
frequent, with examples taken from George Orwell's *Nineteen Eighty-
Four*. They are not meant to prove anything about Orwell's writing,

for which a much fuller survey would be required; it is, however, reasonable to suggest that a good range and variety of connectives is a mark of quality.

1. Conjunctions and conjunctive adjectives such as *however, furthermore, nevertheless*. The appearance of a simple co-ordinating conjunction at the start of a sentence is frowned on by some critics, but in defiance of many acceptable examples:

> If you made unexpected movements they yelled at you from the telescreen. But the craving for food was growing upon him.

2. Pronominal linkage with a preceding noun:

> Winston did not buy the picture. It would have been an even more incongruous possession than the glass paperweight.

3. Repetition of a keyword or proper name, either identically or in a different grammatical form:

> Winston was gelatinous with fatigue. Gelatinous was the right word.
> One day a chocolate-ration was *issued*. There had been no such *issue* for weeks or months past.

4. Use of a synonymous or related word or phrase:

> He knew that *sooner or later* he would obey O'Brien's summons. Perhaps *tomorrow*, perhaps only *after a long delay*—he was not certain.

5. Deictic words—'pointers' like *the, this, that*—either governing a noun or referring back to the whole statement:

> When he came back his mother had disappeared. *This* was already becoming normal at that time.

6. Repetition of opening structure (there was an example of this from Dickens in Chapter 5):

> *He confessed* to the assassination of eminent Party members . . .
> *He confessed* that he had been a spy . . . *He confessed* that he was a religious believer . . . *He confessed* that he had murdered his

H

wife . . . *He confessed* that for years he had been in personal touch with Goldstein.

7. Class-member relationships, or relationship of the parts of a referent to the whole:

Winston picked his way up the lane through dappled light and shade, stepping out into pools of gold wherever the *boughs* parted. Under the *trees* to the left of him the ground was misty with bluebells.

8. Looser semantic connection without repetition of items:

Everything *faded* into mist. The past was *erased*, the erasure was *forgotten*, the lie became truth.

9. Clear sequence of events in successive time:

A hand fell lightly on his shoulder. He looked up.

The other element in division of units is silence: the negative pole of the current, as connection is the positive. The gap on the page, small and unnoticed between sentences, more apparent between paragraphs and unmistakable between chapters and similar large units, corresponds to the breaks in experience of linguistic communication. In all our encounters we find similar short or long vacuities: the pause for breath, the interval for refreshments, the retirement to sleep. No discourse goes on for ever, though the reasons against its doing so are not linguistic. There will be a beginning, intermittent pauses and an end. An apparent exception is found in a work like Joyce's *Finnegans Wake*, starting graphologically half-way through a sentence and ending with the first half of the same sentence, so that reading could begin anywhere and continue indefinitely. But this is a planned deviation, motivated by the Joycean obsession with cyclic return.

The reader will want to attempt his own analysis of texts, encouraged by the fact that there is no rigid system which must be followed. Any examination which increases understanding and response will be worth while. Here, by way of example and not of prescription, is a possible approach to the first two paragraphs of D. H. Lawrence's *Aaron's Rod* (1922). It is not suggested, in this or in other attempts at discourse analysis, that the writer worked out and deliberately incorporated all the features which can be extrapolated from his work. The skilful handling of any medium will develop the best possibilities that the medium contains. Richard Aldington considered this novel to be one of those works of Lawrence which were 'wholly improvisations, begun at random, with no more coherence and structure than the very important ones of Lawrence's compelling personality and brilliant writing'. Helping us to understand what makes for 'brilliant writing' is a function of stylistics.

> There was a large brilliant evening star in the early twilight and underfoot the earth was half-frozen. It was Christmas Eve. Also, the war was over, and there was a sense of relief that was almost a new menace. A man felt the violence of the nightmare released now into the general air. Also there had been another wrangle among the men on the pit-bank that evening.
>
> Aaron Sisson was the last man on the little black railway-line climbing the hill home from work. He was late because he had attended a meeting of the men on the bank. He was secretary to the Miners' Union for his colliery, and had heard a good deal of silly wrangling that left him nettled.

We are not out of order if we take into account information about Lawrence's philosophy and our reading of the whole novel— for intelligent discourse analysis is not likely to follow from the first sentence-by-sentence reading of the text. We can bear in mind the theme of contrast between the individual and society, of a man finding his true self against its pressures.

1. We look at the connectives, identifying them by the numbers already used with the examples from Orwell.

> There was . . . (opening impersonal phrase of situation)
> It was Christmas Eve (semantic and formal link with 'evening' —4)
> Also . . . (conjunction—1)
> . . . the violence of the nightmare . . . (looser semantic link with 'a new menace'—8)
> Also . . . (conjunction—1)
> Aaron Sisson . . . (opens new paragraph, with semantic and formal connection 'men'/'man'—4)
> He was late . . . (pronominal linkage—2)
> He was secretary . . . (pronominal linkage—2)

Thus, looking at the full graphological sentences without seeking their component sentences, we find an interesting distribution of connectives.

2. Parallels of certain features can be seen to link the two paragraphs:

> . . . large, brilliant evening star . . .
> . . . little, black railway line . . .
> (syntagmatic parallels with lexical items in contrast)
> . . . underfoot . . .
> . . . climbing . . .

(loose semantic connection and contrast of items immediately following the parallel structures, setting the individual in the overall scene.)

> . . . wrangle . . .
> . . . wrangling . . .

(formal and semantic parallels link the conclusion of each paragraph).

3. Items from a common semantic area give unity and location:

> . . . pit-bank . . .
> . . . bank . . .
> . . . colliery . . .

4. The single item *man* is twice juxtaposed with its plural form in successive sentences, the first time with impersonal reference and the second time with personal.

5. Words and phrases giving a sense of time are used with semantic contrast:

> 1st. paragraph—evening/early twilight/Christmas Eve/that evening = expectation
> 2nd. paragraph—last man/late = disappointment

6. Syntactic parallels in two successive sentences help to foreground the antecedent item 'Aaron Sisson':

> He was late . . . he had attended . . .
> He was secretary . . . he had heard . . .

7. These features all contribute to the pattern of the two paragraphs which go from the general to the particular, from the

impersonal to the personal, setting the individual 'Aaron Sisson' against the cold, disturbed background.

The first paragraph is built up of sentences whose main verb, stated or concealed, is the past definite *was*:

(i)	there	was	a star
(ii)	(it)	was	early twilight
(iii)	it	was	Christmas Eve
(iv)	the War	was	over
(v)	there	was	a sense of relief
(vi)	that	was	almost a new menace
(vii)	(there)	(was)	a feeling of violence

Item (vii) is the underlying structure of the last sentence, with 'a man' used in an accepted, if now old-fashioned, impersonal sense. The appearance of 'man', however, leads into the changed tense of the next sentence, which is the 'hinge' between the two paragraphs:

there	had been	another wrangle

The second paragraph is dominated by Aaron Sisson as the subject of each sentence; again there is first a sequence of *was*:

Aaron Sisson	was	the last man
	(was)	climbing the hill
	was	late
	was	secretary
	(was)	nettled

but twice the progression is broken with the pluperfect form which switches attention back to the 'wrangle' of the first paragraph:

Aaron Sisson	had	attended a meeting
	had	heard . . . wrangling

This is a simple analysis of a passage from what would by common consent be called a *novel*. While leaving plenty of room for dispute about nomenclature and assignment of particular texts, critics ever since Aristotle have recognized the notion of 'kinds' or 'genres' in literature. These raise their own expectations that must affect the response: they have their own conventions or norms which make further categories within the literary style. The sense of what is proper to a particular genre is by no means confined to classical, medieval or Renaissance criticism, or to the products of a period when notions of 'poetic diction' were dominant.

Here is a vast subject which soon spreads beyond stylistic considerations. But, for example, we accept the use of first-person or third-person narrative in the novel, or the alternation which occurs in a book like *Bleak House*. Continuous second-person address would be considered deviant, though its occasional appearance with direct address to the reader was readily accepted in the fiction of the eighteenth and nineteenth centuries, and regular in the epistolary type like *Humphry Clinker*. It has been extensively used in this century by Beckett and Genet.

We accept that the 'I' of poetry is not always a predication of the poet's 'real' experience or opinion, but may be:

  (i) the imaginary statement of a created character:
      'I am monarch of all I survey'   (Cowper)

 (ii) dramatic statement of the poet's inner experience:
      'I struck the board and cried, "No more!" ' (Herbert)

(iii) a generalized state of mind given particularity:
      'I wake and feel the fell of dark, not day' (Hopkins)

(iv) actual experience narrated, perhaps verifiable from other texts:
      'I wandered lonely as a cloud' (Wordsworth)

and many other things beside.

Again, drama will dispense with the 'he said' type of interpolation required in narrative fiction, while the appearance of dialogue form with characters' names and 'stage directions' in a novel, as in the Nighttown episode in *Ulysses*, is regarded as deviant. In both fiction and drama we not only accept but positively require the shifting of registers in order to differentiate characters and their situations. In poetry the abrupt switch of register causes surprise though (as we have seen) not necessarily condemnation.

Can we go beyond the genre-expectations of a given literature? Our examples have been taken mostly from literature written in English over the last four hundred years—a noble but tiny fragment of the world's literature. To attempt further exploration stretches the resources of stylistics beyond present development. Yet the possibility of quest into regions now obscure is there. Linguists seek continually for the universal principles underlying language as a human activity: schools of comparative literature proliferate. One of the foundation stones of modern linguistics was the discovery of languages different in many essentials from those previously studied by scholars and the realization that valid statements about language cannot exclude any languages which men use.

There are already pioneering efforts, like the work of V. Propp on the folk-tale, classifying plots found in many speech-communities through structure and syntax. Better known, though admittedly controversial, is the comprehensive vision of Claude Lévi-Strauss, an anthropologist who has been much influenced by Saussurean linguistics. He seeks a common principle in all human thinking, as expressed in myth, custom and ritual—manifestations with which literary critics too have become concerned. Roland Barthes leads the 'semiologists' who seek, and sometimes claim to possess, a key to all human 'signs', not solely in linguistic codes.

Little is yet established; but we may reasonably wonder if the existence of similar 'kinds' in literature widely separated in time and space may not yield some clue through discourse analysis. Some of the kinds named by Aristotle are still viable to-day, and the emergence of epic poetry and dramatic action with dialogue can be traced in cultures of which he knew nothing. It may be that there is an approach to be found through stylistics to fresh understanding of the way in which human beings verbalize their experience.

Conjecture points to the future. For the present, a last word of reminder that the study of larger units must incorporate techniques used on smaller segments, while at the same time introducing new considerations. On whatever scale, and in whatever *langue*, a literary text is always a piece of linguistic performance. And this, like the last page of *Finnegans Wake*, is where we came in. The reader will, I hope, continue his study of literary texts knowing that close reading and dissection do not destroy, but rather enhance, the precious gift of delight.

Further Reading

Various kinds of discourse analysis are carried out in many of the books and articles already recommended. The work of Z. S. Harris mentioned on p. 101 is to be found in *Discourse Analysis Reprints* (The Hague, 1963, Mouton) and is important but not easy.

Good shorter studies are: R. Ohmann, 'Literature as Sentences' (*Chatman: Essays*, pp. 231-8); M. Riffaterre, 'Stylistic context' (*Chatman: Essays*, pp. 431-41); J. McH. Sinclair, 'Taking a Poem to Pieces' (*Fowler*, pp. 68-81); M. A. K. Halliday, 'Linguistic Function and Literary Style: an Inquiry into the Language of William Golding's *The Inheritors*' (*Chatman: Style*, pp. 330-68); F. S. Scott and others, *English Grammar* (London, 1968, Heinemann), pp. 203-11.

On the application of statistics to stylistics see: G. U. Yule, *The Statistical Interpretation of Literary Vocabulary* (London, 1944, Cambridge University Press); and L. Dolezel and R. W. Bailey, *Statistics and Style* (New York, 1969, Elsevier).

C. Lévi-Strauss is best approached through his *Structural Anthropology* (New York, 1963, Basic Books and London, 1968, Penguin Press), especially Chapter 2, 'Structural Analysis in Linguistics and in Anthropology', and Chapter 11, 'The Structural Study of Myth'. A general introduction to his work is E. Leach, *Lévi-Strauss* (London, 1970, Collins); see also G. Steiner, 'Orpheus with his Myths: Claude Lévi-Strauss', pp. 248-60 of *Language and Silence* (Harmondsworth, 1969, Penguin Books).

The work of V. Propp mentioned on p. 111 is not easily accessible in English; a translation of his 'Morphology of the Folk Tale' appeared in the *International Journal of American Linguistics* (The Research Center in Anthropology, Folklore and Linguistics, Bloomington, Indiana, 1958); there is a brief critique of Propp in R. Jakobson, 'Linguistics and Poetics' (*Chatman: Essays*, pp. 323-36).

The more difficult fields of general linguistics which are briefly referred to in the foregoing chapter soon pass beyond the scope of this book. Those who wish to venture farther may start with: J. H. Greenberg, ed., *Universals of Language* (Cambridge, Mass., 1963, Massachusetts Institute of Technology Press); and B. L. Whorf, *Language, Thought and Reality* (Cambridge, Mass., 1956, Massachusetts Institute of Technology Press).

Additional Reading

H. S. Babb, ed., *Essays in Stylistic Analysis* (New York, 1972, Harcourt Brace).

M. W. Croll, *Style, Rhetoric and Rhythm* (Princeton, N. J., 1966, Princeton University Press).

D. C. Freeman, ed., *Linguistics and Literary Style* (New York, 1970, Holt, Rinehart and Winston).

R. Fowler *et al.*, *The Language of Literature* (London, 1971, Routledge and Kegan Paul).

G. Hough, *Style and Stylistics* (London, 1969, Routledge and Kegan Paul).

H. M. Hulme, *Explorations in Shakespeare's Language* (London, 1962, Longmans).

M. Joseph, *Shakespeare's Use of the Arts of Language* (New York, 1969, Columbia University Press).

S. R. Levin, *Linguistic Structures in Poetry* (The Hague, 1962, Mouton).

D. Lodge, *The Language of Fiction* (London, 1966, Routledge and Kegan Paul).

J. Miles, *Style and Proportion* (Boston, 1967, Brown).

A. C. Partridge, *The Language of Renaissance Poetry* (London, 1971, André Deutsch).

T. Sebeok, ed., *Style in Language* (New York, 1960, John Wiley).

L. Spitzer, *Linguistics and Literary History* (Princeton, 1948, Princeton University Press).

S. Ullmann, *Language and Style* (Oxford, 1964, Blackwell).

Index